# THE FIGHT
# FOR THE SKIES

Typhoons of No 183 Squadron marshalled on a runway at Thorney Island and ready to roll. The objective is enemy shipping, to be attacked with rocket projectiles. (IWM CH20540)

# THE FIGHT
# FOR THE SKIES

Allied Fighter Action in Europe and North Africa, 1939–1945

## ROGER A. FREEMAN

CASSELL

**Cassell & Co.**
Wellington House, 125 Strand, London WC2R 0BB

Distributed in the USA by Sterling Publishing Co. Inc.,
387 Park Avenue South, New York, NY 10016-8810

First published 1998
This edition 1999

British Library Cataloguing-in-Publication Data:
A catalogue record for this book is available from the British Library

ISBN 0-304-35298-5

Edited and designed by Roger Chesneau/DAG Publications Ltd

Printed and bound in Great Britain by Hillman Printers (Frome) Ltd.

# CONTENTS

# PREFACE

In the minds of the general public the fighter pilot is probably the most distinguished of modern combatants. The lay view of fighter action is duelling aircraft in the heavens where skill will decide the victor. When this is in the cause of directly defending a nation from attack the fighter pilot becomes venerated as an aerial knight. Thus the trade of fighter pilot is invested with a certain amount of glamour and is a position sought by the majority of aspiring military airmen. This was most certainly the case in the Second World War, but the reality of the situation was a different matter. Many fighter pilots never saw an enemy aircraft and even more who did had no opportunity to engage; nor were the majority of combats decided in man-to-man duels, but rather by position, surprise and technical advantage. Furthermore, the casualty rate of fighter pilots was far from low—it was a bloody business.

The purpose of this book is twofold—to dispel some of the myths and inaccuracies fostered by wartime propaganda and to present an unbiased appraisal of the Royal Air Force and United States Army Air Forces fighter effort against that of Nazi Germany and her European allies. The involvement of Russian, French and other fighter forces is acknowledged but is not part of this study. In sequence with the narrative is a large selection of photographs illustrating men, equipment and action (although the last is limited by the nature of air warfare). Several photographs have been published elsewhere, but in this volume the subjects depicted have been researched in order to give detail that was lacking in the original restrictive wartime captions. The reader will see that, where possible, names, dates, locations and aircraft identities are included in the captions in order to establish historical substance.

A number of published works were used as references in the preparation of this volume, and the reader is directed to the following for more detailed information on fighter activity. For the Royal Air Force the late John Rawlings' *Fighter Squad-rons of the RAF* is an excellent record, as is *Aces High* by Christopher Shores and Clive Williams. Of general historical works, John Terraine's *The Right of the Line* proved a useful reference, and *The Battle of Britain: Then and Now*, edited by Winston Ramsey, covers that period admirably. For detailed information on the main RAF fighters, *Spitfire: The History* by Eric Morgan and Edward Shacklady, *The Hawker Hurricane* by Francis Mason and *The Typhoon and Tempest Story* by Chris Thomas and Christopher Shores are recommended. More about individual aircraft and squadrons can be learned from various Air-Britain publications, which are all of a very high standard. A large number of documents were consulted at the Public Record Office, and much of the caption detail is based on individual squadron logs under AIR27.

For the United States Army Air Forces, references were the official Craven and Cate volumes, the USAAF Statistical Summary and a number of other official publications. A reader requiring more information on Eighth Air Force fighter operations should find the author's four *Mighty Eighth* books useful.

Additionally, considerable help and editorial advice was given by Bruce Robertson, a former editor of Air Ministry journals and an acknowledged authority on the Royal Air Force and its aircraft. Alex Vanags-Baginskis also gave editorial advice in association with the *Luftwaffe* connections. The author also thanks Ian Mactaggart for his photographic expertise and for the use of his archive. Others who gave valued help were Dick Baker, Simon Clay, Bob Collis, Mark Copeland, Barry Jones, Danny Morris, Merle Olmsted, Andy Saunders, Andy Thomas, Chris Thomas and the staff of the Imperial War Museum Photographic Archive, particularly David Parry, Ian Carter and John Delaney. To all I offer my sincere thanks.

**Roger A. Freeman**
**March 1998**

# 1
# WINGED WARRIORS

Literally above the horror of the Western Front in the 1914–1918 War arose the fighter ace, a combatant popularly seen as the successor to the chivalrous knight. Originating in French flying units, an ace was at first a pilot who had brought down five aerial adversaries, and this status was embraced by those seeking national heroes. From the outbreak of hostilities military aviation soon developed into the use of aeroplanes to reconnoitre or attack enemy ground forces and to oppose such flights. Those with the purpose of destroying other aircraft became known as scouts and, later, fighters. The next development was the despatch of fighters by one side to oppose the enemy's fighters. Whatever the military outcome, the aerial actions that resulted were presented in the press as the duelling of braves, a clean, honourable form of warfare in comparison with the mass carnage of the trenches. Folklore held the fighter pilot to be an élite warrior.

Popular beliefs aside, while individual skills were important, military forces quickly recognised that technical advantage was a major factor in the outcome of an air combat. The faster aircraft often dominated, but firepower, rate of climb, manoeuvrability, ceiling and endurance were all important. By the last year of the war the tenets of air fighting had been established which would still hold good in another conflict a quarter of a century on—although this was not at first recognised by some when that time arrived.

During the years following the First World War the general public continued to indulge in the 'duelling aerial knights' fable. However, more acute observers knew that most aerial victories had been achieved by competent pilots in superior aircraft using the element of surprise to attack and then effect a withdrawal. In Britain there was an abhorrence of general military matters following the nightmarish conditions of the war, and with few funds there was little incentive for the Royal Air Force to spur the development of new equipment or, apparently, tactics. Some fighter squadrons were still equipped with wartime-designed aircraft nearly a decade later, albeit that the RAF's doctrine held the aeroplane to be an offensive weapon

and, consequently, the bomber received most of the attention at this time.

After a period of unstable government and economic depression, the German nation, still smarting from the imposed conditions of the 1918 armistice, embraced the National Socialist government of Adolf Hitler. While the conditions of the armistice prohibited the production of military aircraft, a small but technically progressive aircraft industry existed and was buoyed to some degree by Germany having become one of the most air-minded of all nations during the inter-war years. At first Britain and France did not see the Nazi dictatorship as a threat to European peace, if in Germany the administration appeared to go from strength to strength in achievement and popularity. Most disturbing was their investment in re-armament, at first clandestine and then blatantly open. By 1934 the British and French governments were sufficiently disturbed by events to make some preparatory moves towards rearmament. The French had established their *Armée de l'Air* as an independent force the previous year, but indecision as to its role, coupled with political instability, produced a far from satisfactory situation over the next few years.

In Britain some important initiatives to modernise were taken. At this time RAF fighter squadrons were equipped with biplanes which were little more than substantial successors to the late types of the First World War. The best was the Hawker Fury, coming into service from 1931, and this was only some 60mph faster at top speed than the 1918 Sopwith Snipe and its armament, two .303in machine guns, was the same. The Schneider Trophy contests had seen startlingly high speeds obtained by the special designs, and the winning Supermarine floatplane recorded 407.5mph on 29 September 1931. The major factor in this record was the powerful Rolls-Royce engine, and Air Ministry advisers looked towards new fighter designs capable of similar high speeds.

It was calculated that attacking an enemy aircraft with .303-calibre ammunition at 300mph would require 250 strikes in two seconds to effect destruction. This rate of fire could only

HURRICANE (MERLIN)

MORANE 406 (HISPANO 850 H.P.)

CURTISS 75.A. (PRATT and WHITNEY 900 H.P.)

MESSERSCHMITT ME. 109 (D.B. 601).

**Above:** The original players on the Western Front: pages from an early RAF recognition manual illustrating the main British, French and German fighters as of September 1939.

be achieved by an armament of eight guns, and these would have to be positioned in the wings to clear the propeller arc. In November 1934 the Air Ministry issued Specification F.5/34 for an eight-gun monoplane fighter. Near the same date it set up a scientific committee chaired by H. (later Sir Henry) Tizard to explore ways to advance air technology. An immediate interest was the development of detection and location of aircraft by radio methods. Under R. A. Watson-Watt this led to the establishment of a chain of RDF stations in south-east England. RDF, radio direction-finding, was a security cover-name for what would eventually be termed radar.

Compared with activity in the German aviation industry at this time, where the Nazi regime promoted and encouraged technical development, the British and French efforts were laggardly. Even the RAF's winning Schneider Trophy aircraft had only been possible through a private donation of funds. The German general superiority was progressively and rapidly advanced over the five years preceding the outbreak of the Second World War. French military aviation was caught up in a nationalisation programme resulting in belated efforts to modernise. In Britain, while limited governmental encouragement and investment was the major factor in this inadequacy,

the bigotry of some aircraft manufacturers played a part. F.5/34 re-drafts resulted in the Hawker Hurricane and the Supermarine Spitfire, the prototype of the former making its first flight on 6 November 1935. But this had been preceded in the same year by the prototypes of two German monoplane fighters. The first, the Heinkel He 112, had disappointing flight characteristics and the design was re-worked. The second, the Messerschmitt Bf 109, which first flew in May, proved to be an exceptional aircraft. In substance, the designer set out to build the smallest possible airframe around the most powerful engine available. It was soon accepted for the *Luftwaffe*, and some later prototypes were given an operational test in the Spanish Civil War, as were the early Bf 109B models when production deliveries commenced in February 1937. Such were the adjudged qualities of the Messerschmitt that development of the Heinkel fighter was discontinued. Believing it prudent not to rely entirely on one make of fighter, however, the German Air Ministry fostered a design by Focke-Wulf, the prototype being completed in great secrecy and making its first flight exactly three months before Hitler's forces invaded Poland.

Alarmed by the growing strength of Germany's armed forces, Britain made more strenuous efforts to rearm in 1937. The stated numbers of *Luftwaffe* bomber aircraft, though exaggerated, brought a growing concern about air strikes on Great Britain, particularly speculation about a 'knock-out blow'. Fighter production and air defence took on a new urgency, and by 3 September 1939 RAF Fighter Command could muster 747 fighters, of which 347 were Hurricanes, 187 Spitfires and the remainder Gladiator biplanes and twin-engine Blenheim night fighters. At this date the French *Armée de l'Air* had 826 fighters classified as modern, although only some 480 of these were considered front-line, mainly Morane-Saulnier MS 406s and Curtiss Hawk 75s, the latter purchased from the United States. On the same date the *Luftwaffe* possessed 1,087 Messerschmitt 109s, of which 630 were the latest 109E model, affectionately known as the 'Emil'.

In total the Allies may have had superior numbers but none of the aircraft types had the combat prowess of the Messerschmitt. Only the Spitfire equalled the 109E's top speed in level flight, the Messerschmitt being some 30mph faster than the Hurricane and 40–50mph faster than the French types. In climb to altitude it outdid the opposition, and only in turning circle was it markedly inferior to the British and French types. The German fighter had a three-blade, controllable-pitch propeller and direct-injection fuelling for its Daimler-Benz engine, whereas both the Hurricane I and Spitfire I were still fitted with wooden two-blade, two-pitch propellers and carburettors subject to gravitational disturbance. With the three-blade Rotol constant-speed propeller the performance of both British types was markedly improved, but this was not then available from production. However, the most important combat advantage that the Bf 109 possessed over its adversaries was its ability to out-dive them: a speed advantage in a dive was vital in closing for attack and also for evading when pursued. Even the vaunted

eight rifle-calibre gun armament of the British fighters would prove less effective than the two cannon and two machine guns of the Messerschmitt. The machine guns, placed in the engine cowling and synchronised to fire through the propeller arc, avoided the ranging problems inherent with the converging fire of wing-mounted guns. The cannon were wing-mounted, but the pilot could choose to fire these separately or combined with the machine guns. The Bf 109E's endurance was equal to the Spitfire's but not as good as that of the Hurricane, although the *Luftwaffe* relied on the promising twin-engine Bf 110 for long-range fighter requirements. Indeed, the Bf 110C had a top speed equal to that of the Hurricane, and it was anticipated that this Messerschmitt, with its then heavy armament of two cannon and four machine guns, would be able to hold its own in combat with British and French interceptors.

If the *Luftwaffe Jagdflieger* had a superior fighter they also had better tactics, in part because of the practical experience gained by the *Legion Condor* that aided Nationalist forces in Spain. The great advance in speed had highlighted problems in interception and formation control. Better flexibility was obtained by operating in pairs, with the leader carrying out the attack and the second aircraft acting as his guard. The RAF and the *Armée de l'Air* fighter units were still employing formations and interception tactics little different from those of 1918.

The propaganda of all three nations held that their pilots and aircraft were the best and the enemy's vastly inferior. A certain amount of this infiltrated the wiser realms of air force commands, where morale had to be maintained. However, in September 1939, exactly how the performances of the main fighter types compared was a matter of speculation for even those technically qualified to judge. Little information was forthcoming from Poland, where most of that nation's aircraft were destroyed on their bases and those brave individuals who took on the Messerschmitts had little success with the obsolete types they flew.

**Right:** The eight-gun fighter. Cases cascade from Spitfire I N3072, of No 611 Squadron, during a butts test firing at Digby in December 1939. The .303-calibre Browning was rated at 1,350 rounds per minute. (IWM C409)

# 2
# THE LULL
# BEFORE THE STORM

The British expectation of an immediate air assault on their homeland did not materialise. Weaknesses in air defence control were quickly realised when on 6 September a false warning of approaching raiders caused a section of Spitfires mistakenly to attack two Hurricanes, shooting them down. A number of lessons were learned the hard way from the chaos of the so-called 'Battle of Barking Creek', primarily improved communications in fighter control and greater emphasis on aircraft recognition training.

The yardstick of strength assessment in RAF Fighter Command was squadrons, and there were 37 in being at the outbreak of war, of which fourteen were Auxiliary Air Force units, originally manned by part-time personnel. Hurricanes equipped eighteen squadrons and eleven had Spitfires. The remaining squadrons were five with the fighter version of the Blenheim light bomber, two with Gladiators and one with Gauntlets, the last two types being biplanes. The authorised complement of a fighter squadron at this time was sixteen aircraft but the day-

**Opposite page:** Hand-cranking the inertia starter on a Hurricane I at Rouvres, France. This is an aircraft of No 73 Squadron, which with No 1 Squadron constituted the fighter element of the Advanced Air Striking Force, with the requirement of providing defence for this formation's Battle and Blenheim squadrons. The fixed, two-blade propeller limited performance at a time when the opposition had three-blade, variable-pitch propellers. (IWM C742)

**Right:** Pilots of No 87 Squadron exhibit a wing panel taken as a trophy from an He 111 shot down by the squadron in November 1939. No 87 was based at Lille-Seclin airfield with No 85 Squadron and formed the 60th Wing of the RAF's Air Component of the British Expeditionary Force, which was charged with the support and protection of the Army. Two former Auxliary Air Force squadrons, Nos 607 and 615, with Gladiators, moved to France in November 1939 for similar duties, forming the 61st Wing. The Auxiliary Air Force, 'the weekend airmen', was incorporated in the RAF at the outbreak of war. (IWM C456)

to-day number on strength varied considerably. The despatch of a British Army Expeditionary Force to France required the RAF to supply a fighter contingent for air defence. The Army, pressing for as many as ten squadrons for this purpose, was strongly opposed by Air Marshal Hugh Dowding, Fighter Command's chief, who did not consider that there were sufficient squadrons to defend Great Britain, even without such detachments. In the event only four Hurricane squadrons were despatched to France, later reinforced by two of the former Auxiliary squadrons with Gladiators. As the Gladiator had a top speed not far removed from that of the enemy bombers it might have to intercept and was actually slower than the Do 17 and

**Right:** King George VI decorates 34-year-old Squadron Leader Andrew D. Farquhar, CO of No 602 (City of Glasgow) Squadron, with the DFC, March 1940. With No 603 (City of Edinburgh) Squadron, the other Scotland-located former Auxiliary Air Force fighter unit, No 602 was charged with the defence of the Firth of Forth area from the early days of the war. The first engagements with the *Luftwaffe* over Britain were made by these Spitfire squadrons, Farquhar sharing in the claim for shooting down a Ju 88 on 16 October 1939 when nine such aircraft of *I/KG 30* attempted to attack naval vessels. The following February he brought down two He 111s, the second aircraft crash-landing near St Abb's Head. Suspecting that the crew would set light to the aircraft, Farquhar attempted to intervene by landing nearby. On touching down his Spitfire nosed over and Farquhar had the ignominious experience of being helped out of the up-ended cockpit by the *Luftwaffe* crew. (IWM C819)

**Right:** The most successful of the Hurricane pilots flying from French bases was a New Zealander, 21-year-old Flying Officer Edgar 'Cobber' Kain of No 73 Squadron. His first success was the downing of a reconnaissance Do 17P on 8 November 1939, and in the following March he became the first RAF fighter pilot of the war to claim five enemy aircraft destroyed. By the end of May, as the last remaining pilot of the squadron who had moved with it to France, his credits of enemy aircraft shot down stood at 16. After take-off from Echemines he made a low-level pass across the airfield and was killed in the crash following a wing-tip striking the ground. The photograph was taken at Rouvres, a few days after Kain (left) claimed his first Me 109E on 2 March and had to crash-land near Metz because his own aircraft had been badly shot up. The other pilot is Sergeant D. A. Sewell, who also had to crash-land his Hurricane after its radiator had been holed in the same air action. (IWM C879)

**Below:** Twenty-six-year-old Flight Lieutenant Peter W. Townsend with pet dog outside No 43 Squadron's caravan at Wick, late February 1940. At the time he had been responsible for bringing down one He 111 and sharing in the destruction of another. Promoted and given command of No 85 Squadron in May, he was eventually credited with the destroying nine enemy aircraft. A charming individual, he was appointed Equerry to HM King George VI in 1944, which led to his name being linked with HRH Princess Margaret, an association unacceptable to the establishment. The other Wick-based Hurricane squadron for the defence of Scapa Flow at this time was No 111; L1822/ JU:K, one of its aircraft (shown), is recorded as participating in shooting down three Me 110s over France in May 1940. (IWM CH101)

Ju 88, this assignment may be seen as a move to placate the generals without seriously weakening the British air defences.

In the eight months of what became known as the 'Phoney War' to the British and *'Sitzkrieg'* to the Germans, with the two sides facing each other from across the Maginot and Siegfried Lines, the air actions were no more than a series of skirmishes. Hurricane and MS 406 pilots made claims of Messerschmitts shot down, and some were, although those of aircraft that supposedly fell in enemy-held territory could not be verified. If the Allied pilots thought they were able to deal with the enemy fighters there was the sombre evidence of losses to their own side. In fact, the true picture was approximately two French or British fighters lost for every Me 109. (The term 'Me 109' was by then being used exclusively by the Allies and to some extent by the Germans themselves.)

It was not so much the inferior performance of the Allied fighters that brought these losses but the tactics used by the opposition. With the advantage of higher altitude, the *Luftwaffe*

**Below:** An attempt to bring down an enemy seaplane while on a shipping foray off Great Yarmouth on 2 April 1940 brought return fire that wounded Hurricane pilot Flying Officer David Phillips in the thigh, causing him to crash-land L1951/TM:L in a field at Martham while part of a No 504 Squadron detachment operating from Wattisham. This was the unit's first encounter with enemy aircraft. The following account of the action was recorded by Pilot Officer Michael Royce, whose brother, Flight Lieutenant William Royce, led the flight involved: 'Two aircraft from Red Section were sent on patrol at 0545 hours and were informed that two bandits were approaching from the east. At 0620 hours Blue Section [Flight Lieutenant Royce, Pilot Officer Phillips and Pilot Officer Royce] went out on convoy patrol. After patrolling at 1,500 feet over the convoy for three-quarters of an hour Blue Section was given Vector 320 and then told to patrol Smith's Knoll Lightship. Red Section were already on patrol there at 3,000 feet and three Spitfires also arrived for five minutes or so. At 07.15 Squadron Leader Hartley Watson was told to pancake and two minutes later Flight Lieutenant Royce spotted two aeroplanes flying echelon port approaching Smith's Knoll from the south. Blue Section, who were flying in search formation, closed up to V formation and dived to investigate. The two aircraft sighted the Section and dived steeply practically to sea level, turning east at the same time. By this time Blue Section were near enough to recognise [that] the two aircraft were Heinkel He 115 float planes . . . As soon as the aircraft had been recognised Blue Section changed into line astern and manoeuvred for position. Flight Lieutenant Royce ordered "Echelon Port, Port Go" and the section swooped to attack. As there were only two aircraft Blue 3 [Pilot Officer Royce] was forced to drop back behind Blue 2 [Flying Officer Phillips] and, when Blue 1 and Blue 2 had finished their attack, to deliver a No 1 attack on the left enemy aircraft of the formation. B1 and 2 pressed home the attack, starting a fire at 250 yards and closing to less than 100 yards. Tracer bullets could be seen leaving the turrets of the enemy aircraft, but after a while the gunner in the leading enemy aircraft was silenced. Blue 1 and 3 both delivered further No 1 attacks, exhausting their ammunition. Both gunners in the enemy aircraft were silent during the second attack. When all the ammunition was exhausted Flight Lieutenant Royce gave the signal to re-form and it was realised that B2 [Flying Officer Phillips] was missing. Flight Lieutenant Royce and Pilot Officer Royce searched the sea for half an hour in a vain attempt to locate Flying Officer Phillips and the ground station, Kiwi, could get no reply to his repeated "Are you receiving me". Just as Flight Lieutenant Royce was giving up the search he was told by the R/T that B2 had force-landed north of Yarmouth. It was later learnt that, in breaking away from his attack, a stray bullet had struck the wireless plug and penetrated his leg, from where it has since been extracted. Flight Lieutenant Royce and Pilot Officer Royce returned to Martlesham Heath and landed to find not a bullet hole or mark on their machines.' The two He 115Bs were from *3/Ku.Fl.Gr. 506;* both had sustained damage and one gunner was wounded. The pilot of S4+EL, *Oberleutnant* Erwin Birking, which was hit in both engines, was forced to attempt a sea landing but the aircraft crashed and sank. He and his crew were rescued. As for Phillips' little-damaged Hurricane, it was soon flying again, finally coming to grief in a hedge at Chipping Sodbury while serving with No 9 Flying Training School. (IWM HU69946)

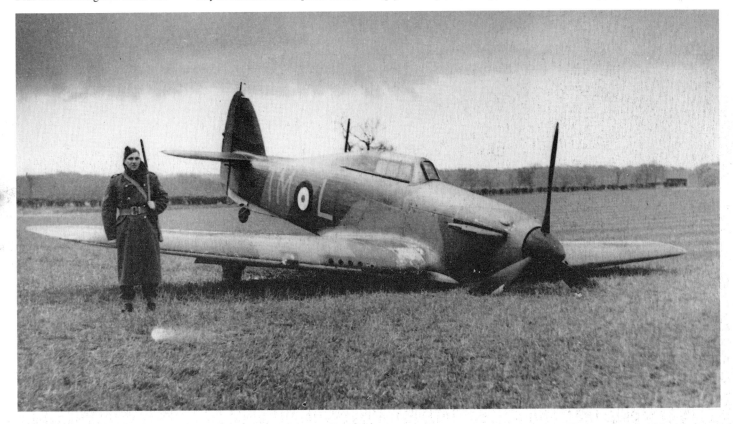

fighters would seek to place themselves up-sun of their adversaries, come down to attack and then dive away to re-form. There was nothing new in this tactic, it having been practised by both sides in the Western Front air battles of the First World War. The Me 109, with its ability to out-dive all the opposition, was an ideal vehicle for such employment. What its wise pilots soon learned to avoid was circling fights, for the Hurricane and most of the French types did not have difficulty in out-turning the 109. The Hurricanes could usually only best the Me 109s with the advantage of surprise or in a turning fight. The British fighter was popular with its pilots, being dependable and having no serious vices, but the airframe was basically a monoplane version of Hawker's successful biplanes and was to some degree outdated when put into production.

RAF pilots had been tutored in what was known as Fighting Area Attacks, with the emphasis on maintaining formation and an orderly follow-the-leader. The leaders' directions were commonly conveyed by hand signals, which, for visual purposes, required close-knit formations. Such set-piece arrangements were soon found highly vulnerable to the enemy's dive, strike and away tactics. The French often flew follow-the-leader columns with the last man detailed to conduct a special look-out for enemy interception from the rear by rolling one wing high and then the other, back and forth, to aid his watch. RAF Hurricane squadrons took up this idea, the 'tail-end Charlie' being the 'weaver'. Even so, the string formation was far more vulnerable to interception than the broad front of pairs used by the *Luftwaffe*. The usual RAF squadron formation was based on three-plane 'V' flights, stacked down behind the leader who could easily be observed. This had been practised with little change since the First World War, but the Hurricane squadrons now found it necessary to space the flights more widely and stacked up away from the sun to minimise surprise from that quarter. The choice of formation used was generally an individual squadron decision and some Hurricane squadrons preferred flying three flights of four aircraft each in line astern with the number four man in each acting as the weaver.

In April 1940 Hitler sent his forces into Denmark and Norway and the British unwisely sent a force to oppose the latter. The Royal Navy may have had a commanding strength at sea but it did not have the necessary protective fighter screen to make this expedition viable. A squadron of Gladiators was sent by carrier to operate from the frozen Lake Lesjaskog and offer some defence against *Luftwaffe* bombers. Quickly overwhelmed, the squadron personnel withdrew to acquire more Gladiators and return to operate from airfields further north. A few days later a squadron of Hurricanes was flown off HMS *Glorious* to expand air defence. After a brief stay in which eleven enemy aircraft were claimed, the squadron was withdrawn, managing successfully to land all serviceable Hurricanes back on board *Glorious*. This skilful achievement was in vain for some hours later this carrier was sunk. Inadequate air cover was a major factor in the failure of this ill-starred campaign.

**Left:** Flight Sergeant Geoffrey Allard of No 85 Squadron being congratulated at Lille-Seclin for bringing down two He 111s on 10 May 1940. 'Sammy' Allard went on to make several claims during the Battle of Britain flying with the same squadron, and by early September, when the squadron was withdrawn from action in the south, he had credits for 19 enemy aircraft destroyed plus five shared with other pilots. No 85 Squadron's N2319/VY:P was one of many Hurricanes lost in France during the next hectic few days. Allard, a colourful character, lost his life in a Douglas Havoc crash at Kirton-in-Lindsey on 13 March 1941 when an improperly secured nose inspection panel became detached after take-off and fouled the tailfin. (IWM C1512)

# 3
# BLITZKRIEG

On 10 May 1940 the *Wehrmacht* offensive in the west was launched, avoiding the main Maginot Line defences by striking through the Ardennes forests into Belgium. Better equipped, trained and led than their opponents, the German forces proved unstoppable. The *Luftwaffe* was an integral part of this 'lightning war', with clear tactical support for the Army wherever it was needed. Above all was an air umbrella of Me 109s drawn from 1,100 serving ten *Jagdgeschwader*. The *Geschwader* was not unlike an army regiment, at this time normally composed of a *Stab* (headquarters unit), and three *Gruppen* each with three *Staffeln.* The *Gruppen* operated independently and were the principal operational units, although for tactical reasons *Staffeln* were sometimes separated. The *Staffel* was the near-equivalent to an RAF squadron, having a complement of a dozen fighters.

An immediate counter by the RAF was the despatch of four additional Hurricane squadrons to France; later, others were commited, to return to their English bases each day after a period of patrol and combat. Many Hurricanes were by then fitted with three-blade, adjustable-pitch propellers to improve performance. Even so, this hardy fighter was still no assured match for the Me 109E, if at the time RAF pilots firmly believed that they could hold their own with this adversary. Experience had also seen the harmonisation of armament altered so that fire converged at 250yds rather than the 400yds originally advised: the closer the contact, the more likely the kill. Combats were often at low altitudes, where the Hurricane's superior turning circle could be employed to advantage. Pilots of the French-based squadrons each flew four or five sorties a day as the German advance continued, with patrols usually at flight strength of three or four aircraft. Not only were the British and French fighters hard put in air fighting, their forward bases were frequently strafed and bombed by the *Luftwaffe*, which attacked 72 airfields on the first day of the campaign. In the first ten days of the *Blitzkrieg* the RAF had some 75 Hurricanes shot down and approximately 130 destroyed on the ground.

The evacuation of British forces from Dunkirk concentrated air activity in this area between 27 May and 4 June, when the *Luftwaffe* was given the task of stemming the rescue operation. Fighter Command put up near-continuous patrols at one- or two-squadron strength, which for the first time brought Spitfires into combat with the Messerschmitts. Although the Spitfire proved equal to or faster than the Me 109E in level flight at medium and low altitudes, the German pilots found that their new adversary could be bested by using the 'Emil''s superior high-altitude performance to make a diving attack and continue down, as the British fighter could be comfortably outdived if pursuing. These combats provided both sides with experience that aided evaluation of the respective types. By the time the evacuation was completed on 4 June nearly all RAF fighter squadrons had seen action over the Channel. Losses and the intense activity brought withdrawal from south-coast stations after only a few days and replacement by unblooded units. In nine days Fighter Command lost 99 aircraft, 42 of which were Spitfires, for claims of 262 of the enemy, which was all but double the true *Luftwaffe* losses. When France capitulated on 22 June 1940 the previous six weeks' fighting had cost the RAF 386 Hurricanes and 67 Spitfires. During the same period the *Luftwaffe* lost 1,279 aircraft, of which 193 were Me 109s and 107 Me 110s. No sound figure is available for French, Belgian and Dutch losses, which were at least 600 aircraft both in the air and on airfields. In total the Germans claimed 4,233 enemy aircraft, of which 1,850 were destroyed on the ground.

The claims of all sides were highly exaggerated, and no doubt as to their authenticity was ever expressed in public by the claimant's side, for the larger the score the better the propaganda value and the effect on national morale. While there were undoubtedly fighter pilots who were economical with the truth, when it came to combat victories, the majority claimed in good faith. The nature of air combat, the speed of action, the excitement, the apprehension and the restricted view from a small cockpit all worked against accurate reporting. It was a

**Left:** No 615 Squadron was sent to France to reinforce the Air Component in November 1939, converting from Gladiators to Hurricanes in the following April. The unit was overwhelmed by the strength of the *Luftwaffe* when the *Blitzkrieg* was launched in May, and within two weeks over half its strength was gone. This shot-down Hurricane, P2907/KW:8, was left for the *Luftwaffe* in a field at Arras. (IWM HU38422)

**Left:** French pilots fought valiantly during the dark days of May and June 1940. Records of their successes are few, although an overall estimation of air victories achieved by *Armée de l'Air* pilots is put at 900, of which 300 were single- and twin-engine fighters. Their most successful pilot was *Lieutenant* Edmond Marin la Meslée, who was credited with sixteen enemy aircraft. He and all but two of the eleven pilots claiming ten or more victories flew the American-made Curtiss Hawk 75A. This 280mph Bloch MB 151 was no match for the Me 109E. (IWM HU38420)

fact that many apparently doomed aircraft survived while others appearing only to have sustained damage never returned to base. The installation of cameras which operated automatically when guns were fired was a significant step in eliminating wishful claims, but these were not yet commonplace. Even so, the assessment of gun camera film could be in error.

If the *Jagdgruppen* had proved superior to their foes during the *Blitzkrieg*, by the time of the French capitulation most had a dwindling number of serviceable fighters and support elements. All but those of a single *Jagdgeschwader* were in late June withdrawn to rear bases to recuperate, soon to return to give cover to *Luftwaffe* bombers which were turned to harassing British shipping in the Channel.

Anti-shipping operations had been undertaken by the *Luftwaffe* from the outbreak of war, with bombing forays on naval vessels at Scapa Flow, in the Firth of Forth and in the North Sea. RAF Fighter Command's response to these raids, conducted by He 111s and Ju 88s, resulted in several interceptions. The first German aircraft brought down on British soil was a Heinkel damaged by Spitfires on 28 October 1939. Following the fall of France a directive issued to the *Luftwaffe* at the end of June 1940 specifically charged it with a campaign of attacking merchant shipping, the Royal Navy, ports and harbours, to cut off Great Britain from her lifeblood of overseas supplies. If it were successful, such action could, it was felt, eventually cause the British to sue for peace. Channel-area attacks on shipping and ports would lure RAF fighters into the air, giving Messerschmitt 109s and 110s the chance to engage and eventually bring about the destruction of Fighter Command. Several *Jagdgruppen,* having returned to the Pas de

Calais area, pursued this policy with some measure of success during July. The British fighters sent to intercept bombers harassing Channel convoys found Me 109s waiting to come down on them.

Although the *Luftwaffe* lost 279 aircraft against the RAF's 142 during the six weeks from 1 July, 128 of the latter were fighters whereas the Me 109 units lost 85. The attrition caused Fighter Command to avoid challenging *Luftwaffe* fighter sweeps from late July and, owing to shipping losses, Channel convoys were largely discontinued. When possible Spitfires were usually sent to engage the Messerschmitts while Hurricanes went for the bombers, but the German fighters invariably had an advantage in altitude. An action on 19 July, when seven Defiants out of a formation of nine were shot down by Me 109s, brought about consideration of the withdrawal of this type from daylight operations within the range of enemy fighters. A similar action in May had seen all but one of a six-plane Defiant formation shot down, and while the two Defiant squadrons had claimed success on other occasions it was clear that the type was quite unsuited for fighter-to-fighter combat. This Boulton Paul design was a two-place, all-metal, Merlin-engine monoplane, featuring a four-gun power turret situated behind the pilot's cockpit. The concept offered greater flexibility in positioning to attack and concentrating the gunner's four .303 Brownings on an enemy aircraft, but in practice it was found that unless the pilot held a steady course it was extremely dif-

ficult for the gunner to hit his target. Moreover, having no fixed forward-firing armament, the Defiant was at a great disadvantage if enemy fighters were encountered. The type also had a poor serviceability record.

Hitler then contemplated an invasion of Britain, a prerequisite being the elimination of RAF Fighter Command. At the beginning of August an assault plan was issued under the codename *Adlerangriff* (Eagle Attack), which required the *Luftwaffe* to bring the RAF to battle in the air and bomb airfields, radar stations and the ground infrastructure targets in south and southeast England. At this time the *Luftwaffe* had assembled for this campaign approximately 1,200 medium bombers (He 111s, Do 17s and Ju 88s) and 400 dive-bombers (Ju 87 *Stukas*) in France and the Low Countries, with fighter support from 800 Me 109s and 280 Me 110s. There were also some 140 He 111s and Ju 88s with 30 Me 110s that could be used to attack north-east Britain from bases in Norway and Denmark. Against these forces RAF Fighter Command had just over 600 aircraft in squadron service. The *Luftwaffe* was generally confident of success—understandably so following its ascendancy during the May/June *Blitzkrieg*.

**Below:** Chain Home radar stations were established along the south and east coasts of Britain in the late 1930s and provided an invaluable early warning of high- and medium-altitude raiders' approach. Each steel tower was 360ft high. This is the Chain Home site at Poling, Sussex. (IWM CH15173)

# 4
# THE BATTLE OF BRITAIN

**B**ritain's defences against air attack had received reasonable attention over the past five years. As daylight bombing was the major anticipated threat, the interceptor fighter was considered the main weapon of defence. By August 1940 the country was divided into four Fighter Command areas, each having a Group headquarters controlling the fighter airfields and their squadrons within its area. No 10 Group covered the south-west counties of England, No 11 the south-east around London, No 12 the middle band of the country and No 13 northern England and Scotland. Each Group had so-called Sectors, control centres on selected airfields which had direct operational control of airborne squadrons and vectored them on to enemy aircraft. The early warning from the RDF stations (by then known as Chain Home) and Observer Corps' visual trackings were fed to the command and sector centres, enabling fighters to be airborne and positioned to meet an incoming raid.

*Luftwaffe* bombers had been conducting small-scale night raids over Britain since 5 June, mostly against airfields and ports. At the beginning of August bombers were also sent out in daylight. In poor weather, when cloud gave protection, these were usually harassing attacks by single aircraft against airfields or communications targets. In good weather small formations of up to 30 bombers with heavy support from fighters attacked south coast ports when, it was hoped, Spitfires and Hurricanes would arrive to intercept. Thus began the aerial onslaught of high summer 1940 which came to be known as the Battle of Britain, although *Adlerangriff* proper was not launched until 13 August. Then more than a thousand *Luftwaffe* sorties were flown, chiefly against airfields, and, after the weather had restricted activity the next day, double this sortie figure on the 15th when attacks were also made on targets in north-east Britain. The first of these major offensives brought the *Luftwaffe* a loss of 20 bombers plus fourteen rated severely damaged, 24 fighters destroyed and six badly damaged. Against this Fighter Command lost fourteen aircraft shot down and six badly damaged. Of the German fighters, fifteen were twin-engine Me 110s which, despite their speed and heavy armament, were shown generally to be no match for the British interceptors. On the 15th, apart from seeing the highest number of sorties, the *Luftwaffe* also suffered its highest losses for one day in all its operations over Britain— total of 70. For the first and last time it involved a major effort by *Luftwaffe* forces based in Norway and Denmark. The He 111s and Ju 88s, es-

**Left:** No 611 Squadron Spitfire Is in a set-piece, follow-my-leader attack column, common practice for Fighter Command units in the first year of hostilities. It took some time for its vulnerability to be appreciated, in that an enemy interceptor was presented with one target after another as he flew down the line. (IWM CH737)
**Right:** Squadron Leader Peter Townsend unbuckles as ground crew personnel prepare to replenish fuel and oxygen. The CO of No 85 Squadron had just returned to the forward base at Martlesham Heath from a convoy patrol off the East Anglian coast during the second week of July 1940. On 31 August 1940 Townsend had to abandon this Hurricane, P3166/VY:Q, over Hawkhurst, Kent, when it was badly shot up and he was wounded in the foot. He had previously shot down an Me 109E and damaged another. (IWM HU73457)

**Right:** The crew aboard, ground men prepare to aid starting Defiant L7021/PS:H at Martlesham Heath during the second week of July 1940. On 28 August this aircraft was shot down by an Me 109 over Faversham, Kent, the crew managing to bale out. No 264 Squadron's third CO, Squadron Leader George Garvin, landed safely but his gunner, Flight Lieutenant Robert Ash, was dead, possibly hit by bullets during his descent. (IWM HU73461)

corted by Me 110s, sought ports and airfields in north-east England, losing fifteen and seven respectively of their number to Hurricanes, which suffered damage but no losses.

Another major operation by the *Luftwaffe* on 18 August resulted in losses of 67 German aircraft and 42 RAF, ten of the latter being Hurricanes destroyed on the ground at Kenley. Of the German losses, eighteen were Ju 87s and fourteen Me 110s, which meant that nearly a quarter of the dive-bomber strength and a third of the so-called *Zerstörer* had been dissipated in ten days of fighting. Such losses were prohibitive, and thereafter the units with these types were only commited to battle when fighter interception was deemed a more limited risk or when strong Me 109 support was provided. The *Stuka* had proved an excellent vehicle for accurate dive-bombing during both the Polish and western *Wehrmacht* campaigns, but this was when *Stuka* units were able to go about their mission with little aerial opposition. Slow, relatively cumbersome and with a single machine gun for rear defence, the Ju 87 had little chance of survival when set upon by Hurricanes or Spitfires. As for the Me 110, this was a particular disappointment to the *Luftwaffe* as, with a top speed near that of the Hurricane and a heavy armament of two 20mm cannon and four rifle-calibre machine guns, it was expected to provide long-range escort for the bombers. High speed and an excellent gun platform were insufficient qualities to match against modern single-seat fighters with superior acceleration, climb and manoeuvrability—in fact, the Me 110 proved as vulnerable to interception as the bombers it was supposed to protect. Once aware of this situation, Me 110

*Staffeln* at times would form a defensive circle where each aircraft covered the tail of that in front. This, generally, provided only limited protection for the more nimble Hurricanes and Spitfires could usually break up the circle.

By mid-August German Intelligence estimated Fighter Command losses at about 800 fighters, which was roughly $2^1/_2$ times the actual number. For that matter, British claims of German aircraft shot down were averaging more than twice as many as actually fell; over-claiming continued common to both sides. While the *Luftwaffe* High Command believed their forces were succeeding in reducing Fighter Command to a critical state, even if the cost was high, the reality was that they were nowhere near their goal. Hard-pressed though the British squadrons were, they were still able to put 600 fighters into the air. The RAF had an excellent recovery and repair service which put many crash-landed fighters back into service in an amazingly short time.

While the Germans knew that Fighter Command had a control system it appears that they did not fully appreciate the coordination of radar sites, Observer Corps reporting and the sector control rooms which plotted and directed the fighter squadrons. Although the destruction of Fighter Command was the main objective of the offensive, much of the effort was dissipated by attacks on unconnected targets, suggesting poor intelligence appraisal. Many of the airfields bombed did not serve fighter squadrons. Cloud forced some formations to seek targets of opportunity and bombs were scattered over the English countryside. The Chain Home radar sites had received some attention, but the *Luftwaffe* concluded that these large masts and adjacent protected buildings were difficult targets to destroy, particularly so if the precision of the *Stuka* could not be utilised.

Attacks on airfields continued during the rest of August with smaller bomber formations shepherded by much larger numbers of fighters, the purpose to involve the British fighters in combat and so erode their numbers. During this period the *Luftwaffe* continued to embrace highly inflated totals of British losses, but the true picture, if then unknown to both sides, was that for every Me 109 that fell Fighter Command lost one and a half aircraft. The scale of the fighting fluctuated from day to day, and on average Fighter Command was losing the equivalent of one squadron of pilots and two squadrons of air-

**Left:** Pilot Officer Albert Lewis gets ready to board Hurricane P2923/VY:R of No 85 Squadron at the Debden satellite airfield of Castle Camps, 25 July 1940. A South African, Bert Lewis had fought with No 85 during the May *Blitzkreig* and claimed nine enemy aircraft. He had further victories with Nos 85 and 249 Squadrons during the Battle of Britain for a grand total of 18 before being shot down himself on 27 September, suffering extensive burns. On recovery he was sent to Ceylon, where he was again shot down and wounded, thereafter, as far as is known, taking no further part in operations. Hurricane P2923 was missing in action on 18 August 1940 with Flight Lieutenant Richard H. A. Lee, another able pilot, said to have achieved nine victories. (IWM HU73458)

ready to execute the usually fruitful diving attacks on the British fighters as they came in on the bombers—unlike close escorts, which had to fly at reduced speed and zigzag to stay with the bombers, and so to a certain extent render themselves vulnerable to attack. The top cover flew high-speed ranging patrols, allowing these aircraft to engage their enemy quickly; if then finding themselves pursued, they could use their superior acceleration and diving speed to break off combat.

The British were also having to evolve new tactics while engaged in this relentless battle. Fighting Area Attacks had quickly been abandoned and individual squadrons with command advice worked out their own tactics. These were diverse and included mass frontal attacks on bomber formations. Many British pilots did not fully appreciate either the technical or the tactical advantages of their enemy. Others who lived long enough began to dispense with the three-plane flight and emulate the opposition with the more flexible leader and a 'No 2' as weaver. Nor was the futility of breaking off combat to dive away from an Me 109 clearly understood by some pilots—or the most successful evasive action of, if possible, turning to meet the attack.

Usually no more than one or two squadrons 'scrambled' (RAF slang for hurried despatch to combat) to meet a reported plot of an incoming enemy formation. While this policy con-

craft every day. It so happened that the aircraft losses were not yet crucial owing to new production, reserve holdings and repairs. Pilots were another matter, for many of the most experienced men had been killed or seriously wounded. Hastily trained replacements were far more vulnerable in combat and thus accelerated the rate of losses. However, a similar situation faced the *Luftwaffe*.

RAF losses were heightened by making the destruction of enemy bombers the main aim, which often involved diving through the enemy escort that would follow with the advantage of overtaking speed. Moreover, many raids had an accompanying formation of high-flying, free-roving Me 109s

**Right:** At 36, Irishman Wing Commander Victor Beamish was one of the oldest pilots flying fighters in the Battle of Britain. This did not stop him from claiming several enemy aircraft while station commander at North Weald during that fateful summer. Much of his flying was with No 151 Squadron. After a staff post at No 11 Group he returned to North Weald, frequently participating in operations. In March 1942 he was posted missing in action, his Spitfire believed shot down by an Me 109. He is seen here in July 1940, right, with Squadron Leader Edward M. Donaldson, CO of No 151 Squadron, famed for achieving a world speed record of 610mph in a Meteor post-war. (IWM CH490)

served the force, holding other squadrons on the ground to intercept other possible raids, one or two squadrons were often inadequate to deal with sizeable enemy formations. Thus on 26 August Air Vice-Marshal Park, No 11 Group's commander, issued a requirement for the leaders of squadrons to radio the numbers, height and position of the enemy when first making contact so that, if necessary, other squadrons could be vectored to assist. Sometimes the RAF squadrons did not find the enemy formation through arriving at too high an altitude. This was put down to the natural tendency of adding another one or two thousand feet to that given so as to be sure of being above the enemy. As the ground controllers had probably already done a similar reckoning-up for the same reason, a squadron might be as much as 4,000ft above the enemy formation and so fail to see it.

Another area where the British were disadvantaged was in aircraft armament. The fusillade of rifle-calibre bullets from the eight guns of a Hurricane or Spitfire could, if centred on the target, produce decisive damage, but frequently the airframe of an enemy aircraft was peppered with holes which had no lethal effect. Many German aircraft were brought down because crew members were killed or seriously wounded, but this was countered by additional armour protection. On the

**Above:** A section of No 65 Squadron Spitfires taking off from Coltishall at 1715 hours on 12 August 1940. R6714/YT:M was piloted by Pilot Officer Tom Smart and R6712/YT:M by Flight Sergeant Joe Kilner, both of whom had several victories during 1940. As a Squadron Leader, Tom Smart was lost flying from Malta in April 1943; he baled out but his parachute was not seen to open. Joe Kilner survived hostilities, promoted to Squadron Leader. The aircraft had shorter lives: R6714 went out of control near Gateshead, killing Sergeant K. Pearson on 16 October 1940; R6712 was written off in a training accident the following May. Largely hidden in the photograph, the leading Spitfire of the section, R6713, flown by Flight Lieutenant Gerald Saunders, crashed in Kent with another pilot on 18 August 1940. The wartime censor's deletion marks can be seen on airfield aerials in the photograph. (IWM HU54421)

other hand, the damage incurred by the detonation of a single 20mm cannon shell from a German fighter was often sufficient to disable a Hurricane or Spitfire. There was plenty of evidence from wrecks in the English countryside to show clearly the advantage of explosive ammunition and the shortcomings of rifle-calibre strikes. Moreover, when a fighter had to persist with machine-gun fire in order to cripple an enemy bomber fatally, its continued presence gave the bomber's gunners a better opportunity to hit their adversary. In fact, for every five British fighters lost to enemy fighters, one succumbed to bomber defences.

The RAF had toyed with the idea of installing 20mm cannon in its fighters as early as 1936, but the enthusiasts for the

**Right:** One of 20 *Luftwaffe* aircraft that did not return to base on 14 August 1940. He 111P 1G+NT of *9/ KG 27* crashed at Charterhouse in the Mendips after meeting Spitfires of No 92 Squadron's Green Section, Pilot Officers Desmond Williams and Allan Wright. With five enemy aircraft destroyed to his credit, Williams was killed in an air collision two months later. Wright endured to serve in the post-war RAF, retiring in 1967. The wartime censor has deleted the unit markings on the Heinkel's fuselage in the photograph. (IWM CH1887)

battery of .303-calibre Browning machine guns (with twice the rate of fire) prevailed as far as the Spitfire and Hurricane were concerned. The vast reserves of .303 ammunition were a telling factor. Dowding was one of these enthusiasts and saw no advantage in cannon armament. The Westland Whirlwind, a promising twin-engine, single-seat fighter, was to have cannon, although the aircraft's production was delayed chiefly through problems with its Rolls-Royce Peregrine engines. Hurricanes and Spitfires with 'twenty-millimetres' were under experimentation during the early months of hostilities, this work not being pressed until the following summer when service tests were carried out. The Hispano weapons suffered persistent jamming problems which were not quickly resolved.

In a further effort to bring RAF fighters to battle, the *Luftwaffe* turned its attention to London, believing that the RAF would not hesitate to put strong forces into the air to defend the capital and so enable the Me 109 *Jagdgruppen* to use the fighting advantages of their aircraft further to reduce the strength of Fighter Command. Although the Me 109's endurance was in the region of 90 minutes and the flight to the London area would leave only 15 to 20 minutes for combat, with the force available this was not a serious handicap.

The first major daylight raid, with approximately 650 bomber and a thousand fighter sorties, was launched in the afternoon of 7 September, although night bombing had begun two nights earlier as a retaliation raid for the RAF's bombing of Berlin. As expected, RAF fighters did rise to contest the raids of 7 September and in endeavours to check the bombers the 23 squadrons engaged had 28 aircraft shot down, 25 due to Me 109 actions—this against fourteen Me 109s in the total *Luftwaffe* losses of 36 for the day. Unlike most German airmen, RAF pilots who took to their parachutes would fly again, notwithstanding injuries. Some suffered horrific burns as in both the Spitfire and Hurricane the fuel tank was forward of the cockpit. Messerschmitt pilots were less likely to suffer burns as the tank was behind the cockpit.

In the following week London continued to be the main target for the *Luftwaffe*'s attacks, although the weather brought days with comparatively little activity, giving the hard-pressed squadrons of No 11 Group some respite. Nevertheless the attrition continued, which convinced most in the *Luftwaffe* hierarchy that it was only a matter of days before the British would be unable to offer spirited defence in numbers, the bombing of London being the prime bait to bring the Spitfires and Hurricanes to battle. It was still believed that the RAF was being defeated and that air combat was the most profitable means of bringing about its speedy demise. Unfortunately for the *Luftwaffe* their intelligence was wrong in that, although the attrition suffered by Fighter Command during the past three months was certainly critical, the strength of the force and its ability to function effectively was underestimated. Thus on 15 September, when some 300 bombers and 900 German fighters were sent to London while Southampton suffered a diversionary raid,

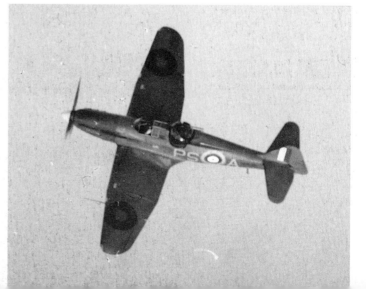

they were met by near 200 British fighters. The results of this conflict gave a sobering blow to the *Luftwaffe*'s confidence. With good direction the RAF squadrons were able to make the day a particularly devastating experience for the bomber *Kampfgruppen*, from which 35 aircraft failed to return and 22 of those that did suffered damage. The experience of the *Jagdgruppen* was also of concern as 23 fighters failed to return to their French bases, and their dismay would have been the more so if at the time their claims made against the enemy had been known to be more than twice that of the RAF's true loss of 26, with many pilots safe to fly again. Thereafter the *Luftwaffe*'s activity by day decreased, partly through inclement weather making successful bombing of targets a dubious proposition. However, the continuing resilience of Fighter Command had clearly indicated to the German High Command that the air superiority deemed essential for a successful invasion of southern England had not been achieved. This failure, together with RAF's bombing of assembled water transport such as barges for troop carrying, a potentially strong reaction from the Royal Navy and the onset of autumn, caused Hitler and his advisers to consider the invasion a doubtful venture and its indefinite potponement was ordered.

Sporadic daylight bomber raids with escort were carried out to the end of September with an overall lessening of attrition in RAF squadrons. This was due in some measure to the improved tactics of the defenders, who by then understood better their opponent's advantages and weaknesses. From the early weeks of the *Luftwaffe*'s daylight onslaught against Britain, where possible the more agile Spitfires had been sent against the Me 109s, leaving the Hurricanes to intercept the bombers. In practice it was not possible to effect this rigidly, so Spitfires at times engaged the bombers and Hurricane pilots found themselves in combat with the Messerschmitts. Endeavouring to conserve his forces, Air Vice-Marshal Park favoured attacking the enemy formations at squadron strength, often with a single Hurricane squadron to tackle the bombers while a squadron of Spitfires fended off the escort. The result was that invariably a dozen RAF fighters would find themselves in combat with three times that number of enemy aircraft, or, more factually, the larger spread of *Luftwaffe* fighters would have a greater opportunity to force the pace of battle and best the opposition with diving attacks. The policy in No 12 Group, under Air Vice-Marshal Leigh-Mallory, was that where possible the intercepting force should be at wing strength of three or four squadrons. Thus some 36 fighters acting in concert were better able to counter the enemy's similarly large formation of fighters. There were some instances where wing assemblies paid off, but generally the Me 109s still had the advantage through their superior high-altitude capability. The maxim that altitude held the advantage was true, particularly when the opposition could be out-dived.

During the height of the offensive the *Luftwaffe* began using Me 109s and Me 110s as fighter-bombers (*Jabos*), a practice

**Below:** Quiet before the storm: a No 264 Squadron dispersal area at Kirton-in-Lindsey during the first week of August 1940. On the 22nd the squadron prepared to re-join the battle, moving south to Hornchurch. A few days after this photograph was taken all three aircraft in view had been shot out of the sky. On the 24th L7013/PS:U was badly damaged by Me 109s and was force-landed at Manston by Flying Officer E. W. Campbell-Colquohoun. L7005/PS:X was crash-landed at Chislet, Kent, on the 26th, and L7026/PS:V crashed at Hinxhill, Kent, on 28 August, the crew being killed. All were victims of Me 109Es. PS:X was flown by the most successful of all Defiant crews, Sergeant Edward Thorn and Sergeant Fred Barker, who were eventually credited with a dozen enemy aircraft, three this day including the Me 109E that shot them down. Thorn and Barker only had minor injuries; the Messerschmitt pilot paid with his life. (IWM CH880)

Right: The opposition. Red 14, the Me 109E flown by Unteroffizier Zaunbrecher of 2/JG 52, demolished several oat traves when crash-landing near Berwick railway crossing, east of Lewes, on 12 August 1940. The results of an RAF pilot's marksmanship can be seen on the rear fuselage and tail. (IWM)

that gradually moved towards the single-seat type carrying a 250kg bomb and flying at altitudes above 25,000ft. The favourite target was London, and, if flying above 30,000ft, aircraft could reach the capital almost with impunity. These raids were of little more than nuisance value, if extremely difficult for the RAF to intercept at this time. Nevertheless, when Spitfires could reach these high altitudes in time the slower, bomb-laden Me 109s proved reasonably vulnerable. When British defences began to exact a growing toll from these sorties, the *Luftwaffe* finally decided little useful purpose was being served and the operations virtually ceased.

The resilience of RAF Fighter Command was the prime cause of Hitler's decision to defer indefinitely an invasion of Britain. Neither aerial opponent was defeated but both were sorely scarred by the attrition of the battle, particularly the loss of experienced aircrew. Aircraft could be and were replaced, although by September the rate of losses did not bode well for the future if they continued at such high levels. Of the lessons learned, the most obvious was that, even with considerable fighter escort and support, it was nearly impossible to deflect determined attacks on bombers by the opposition's fighters. The daylight operation of bombers or other slow-flying aircraft was proved to be a hazardous business. Valour aside, the RAF pilots' achievement in giving the *Luftwaffe* a bloody nose, even if they took two punches for every one of theirs, is all the more creditable in that they fought their more numerous enemy fighters which were superior in performance and armament.

Right: A section of No 54 Squadron Spitfires scrambled at Hornchurch to intercept got no further than the runway when bombs cascaded across the airfield. R6895 crashed inverted and burnt, although the pilot, Flight Lieutenant Alan Deere, managed to escape with only a slightly torn scalp; the pilots of the other two Spitfires destroyed escaped little hurt. Deere became a noted fighter ace, having some 15 destroyed claims during 1940, one made in R6895. (IWM HU70347)

**Left, upper:** Squadron Leader Brian Lane's Spitfire I, in which this newly appointed CO of No 19 Squadron shot down an Me 110 on 7 September 1940 and two more on the 11th of that month. Lane was himself shot down by an Fw 190 and killed during a Rhubarb on 13 December 1942, shortly after taking command of No 167 Squadron. Retired from squadron service, Spitfire P9386 spent three years in a training role, lastly with No 57 OTU, whilst serving with which unit it was written off in a crash in East Lothian on 5 May 1944. (IWM CH1367A)

**Left, lower:** Do 17Z F1+FS of *8/ KG76* was brought down on Castle Farm, Shoreham, on 15 September 1940. One member of the crew was killed and another wounded by the hail of bullets from No 609 Squadron Spitfires, both of whose pilots would die in later combats. (S. Clay Collection)

**Right, top:** A Spitfire of No 66 Squadron on its landing approach to Gravesend on 18 September 1940, a day on which the squadron lost two pilots. The Spitfire in the foreground, R6800/LZ:N, with 'tin hatted' ground staff, is that of the CO, Squadron Leader Rupert Leigh. The Hurricane on the field, R4105/SD:U, is from No 501 Squadron. (IWM HU73459)

**Right, centre:** No 222 Squadron Spitfires leaving Hornchurch on 24 September 1940 for the forward base at Rochford to await their next call to battle. A formation take-off saved time and fuel. The aircraft in the foreground is X4067, issued to No 222 the previous day. It still wears the code letters DW:K of No 610 Squadron, with which it previously served. This Spitfire was shot up by an Me 109 on 24 August, wounding Pilot Officer Donald Gray, who crash-landed near Dover. Repaired, the aircraft was back in the air within a month. (IWM HU69943)

**Right, bottom:** Force-landed with a holed fuel tank, Spitfire I X4177/ UM:A of No 152 Squadron reposes in a meadow at Skew Bridge, Newton St Loe, near Bath, on 25 September 1940. Squadron Leader Peter Devitt led an interception of *KG 55* He 111s raiding Bristol and was hit by return fire. Another No 152 Squadron Spitfire was also brought down, but three of the Heinkels fell in England and a fourth crash-landed in France as a result of battle damage. X4177 was flying again a few weeks later, thanks to the excellent RAF repair and recovery service. (IWM HU69943)

**Above:** The RCAF's No 1 Squadron, renumbered No 401 Squadron on 1 March 1941, took part in the Battle of Britain. One of its Hurricanes, V6609/YO:X, is shown at Castletown in November 1940. Parachutes were placed on the wing to avoid damp and vermin. (IWM CH1723)

**Below:** No 242 Squadron Hurricanes in the standard transit formation used by RAF Fighter Command during the early war years. With the aircraft in three-plane V sections, each following section is stacked progressively down to give pilots a good view of the leader's direction. Early Canadian volunteers for the RAF were originally concentrated in this squadron, which saw much action over France in May 1940. Refurbished at Coltishall during the following month under the famous 'legless' pilot Douglas Bader, No 242 became part of the Duxford 'Big Wing' during the Battle of Britain. This photograph was taken early in October 1940 when the squadron operated from Duxford. The leading aircraft is Squadron Leader Bader's V7467/LE:D, in which he had shot down at least four enemy aircraft the previous month. (IWM CH1430)

**Above:** Armourers preparing to replenish the ammunition bays of a No 312 Squadron Hurricane I at Speke early in October 1940. The second of the three fighter squadrons manned by Czechoslovakian pilots, it spent six months as a guardian of Liverpool. L1926/DU:J was used by Flight Lieutenant Alois Vasatko in bringing down a Ju 88A of *2/KGr* *806* on 8 October 1940, a victory shared with two other pilots. Vasatko already had a distinguished service as a fighter pilot, first in his homeland and then in France, where, flying Curtiss H-75As, he participated in shooting down several *Luftwaffe* aircraft. The following year Vasatko was given command of No 312 and in 1942, as a Wing Commander, the Exeter Wing. He was killed in a collision with an Fw 190 off the Devon coast on 23 June 1942. (CH1434)

**Below:** Repairs to Hurricane P3886/UF:K of No 601 Squadron after an undercarriage failure at Exeter in early October 1940. This venerable aircraft later served with three other squadrons, an OTU and the Merchant Ship Fighter Unit before being packed off to India where it was struck off charge in September 1944. By October 1940 No 601 Squadron was claiming over 100 enemy aircraft destroyed and received ten DFC awards. (IWM CH1638)

**Above:** A squadron seeing little fighting during the main action of the Battle of Britain was No 245, which was sent to Aldergrove in July 1940 and remained in Northern Ireland for over a year. Photographed on 19 November 1940, this flight is led by the CO, Squadron Leader Eric Whitley DFC, in his Hurricane P3101/DX:?, popularly known as the 'CO's Query'. This unusual individual aircraft identification came about the previous year when the squadron was formed and Whitley was undecided as to what letter to use. It was suggested he use a question mark instead of a letter to distinguish the CO's machine. A 'Joker' motif was also carried on the side of the cockpit. P3101 was the second Hurricane with these markings and in later months the idea was taken up in other squadrons where the CO wished to distinguish his personal mount. (IWM HU73456)

**Left:** No 609 has been credited as the second most successful squadron during the Battle of Britain with a total of 48 enemy aircraft destroyed. The squadron's most successful pilot was Flight Lieutenant John Dundas with more than a dozen victories. On 28 November 1940 No 609 became involved in a fighter action near the Isle of Wight, Dundas shooting down the leading Me 109E which was flown by *Major* Helmut Wick, commander of *JG 2* and at the time the *Luftwaffe*'s leading *Experten* with 56 victories. Dundas's success was short-lived, for, like many other RAF fighter pilots during the Battle of Britain, he fell victim to the other member of the *Rotte*, the widely spaced two-plane element employed by the *Jagdflieger*. Both Wick and Dundas are believed to have baled out, but neither was recovered from the sea. (IWM CH2583)

**Right:** Flight Lieutenant John Mungo-Park, in the cockpit of his No 74 Squadron Spitfire, talking to Pilot Officer Harbourne Stephen after they had shared the destruction of an Me 109E in the Dungeness area on 30 November 1940, claimed as the 600th enemy aircraft shot down by fighters operating from Biggin Hill. Stephen, a pre-war journalist, eventually had nine air victories and shared in another eight, all apart from one of the latter achieved in 1940. He rose to the rank of Wing Commander but saw little action after 1941. Mungo-Park had 11 destroyed and two shared victories with No 74 Squadron before failing to return from a sweep on 27 June 1941. (IWM HU73463)

**Right:** The most successful squadron in the Battle of Britain was No 603, flying Spitfires. It claimed 67 enemy aircraft shot down and although on post-war information this was revised to 58 it was still ten more than the runner-up No 609. Pilot Officer Ronald Berry was the squadron ace, with ten victories achieved without any damage to his aircraft. Photographed on 11 January 1941 at Drem after the squadron had returned to the north (it was originally the City of Glasgow Squadron of the Auxiliary Air Force), 'Ras' Berry went on to fly combat in North Africa and by the end of the Tunisian campaign had the considerable record of having shot down 14 enemy aircraft, shared in the destruction of ten and had nine probables, 17 damaged and seven destroyed by strafing. (IWM HU73462)

# 5
# BLITZ

The attrition rendered through daylight operations during high summer 1940 turned the *Luftwaffe's* bombing offensive to the cover of darkness. During the winter of 1940 and into the spring of 1941 from 50 to 500 bombers a night raided Britain's major towns and cities, chiefly the capital. RAF Fighter Command was hard put to shoot down any of the invaders, leaving anti-aircraft artillery, deficient in numbers as it was, to provide the main defence. The fighter version of Blenheim light bomber was the principal night interceptor, for which the first installations of Airborne Interception (AI) radar were made. Although airborne radar held great promise, this equipment was still very much in the experimental stage and did not enter operational trials until the summer of 1940.

During the so-called Blitz night fighters relied principally on good fortune and the good night vision of the crews to shoot down enemy bombers. Vectoring by ground stations was im-precise and in most cases it was nothing less than good luck to be in a position to pick up an enemy aircraft visually in the darkness. Searchlights were the principal aid in that these could be used to indicate the approximate course of an unseen raider. If the enemy were flying below 10,000ft, the useful limit of beam illumination, searchlights could and often did catch and hold a target for a night fighter to attack. Such was the case during the fruitful night of 18/19 June 1940, when six He 111s were brought down at a cost of three Blenheims and a Spitfire. This night provided both sides with useful intelligence: for the

**Below:** The Blenheim IF operated on a limited scale in daylight against *Luftwaffe* bombers, mostly in areas beyond the range of the Me 109. It served as a night fighter from the early days of the war, only to suffer more losses in accidents than its crews made claims of enemy aircraft. Flying from North Weald, this flight of No 25 Squadron aircraft, led by L1437/ZK:P, is on North Sea convoy patrol in April 1940. (IWM HU73455)

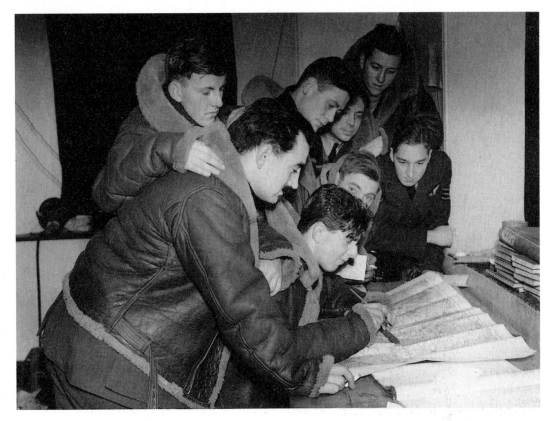

**Right:** Night fighting was a fairly exasperating business for night fighter crews in 1940 as making contact with the enemy in darkness was rare. Experiments with flare dropping to try and illuminate *Luftwaffe* bombers proved unsuccessful. The great hope was airborne radar and the new Beaufighter; meanwhile it was a case of groping in the night with the early, unreliable AI sets. Here a detachment of No 29 Squadron Blenheim air crews studies a map (for the photographer's benefit) in a crew room at Colby Grange, 28 October 1940. At this date the squadron had a dozen claims for enemy aircraft destroyed but had lost as many of its own in night accidents. (IWM CH1582)

*Luftwaffe* that its bombers should operate above 12,000ft in order to avoid searchlights; and for the RAF that prolonged firing contact with enemy bombers increased the risk of return fire, and that in darkness the enemy gunners often saw the intercepting fighter before the fighter pilot saw his quarry.

The Blenheim Mk IF, with its underfuselage 'tray' of four .303in machine guns, was not only inadequately armed for the night fighting task, it was also only marginally faster than the He 111 and Do 17 and slower than the Ju 88. Often when searchlights illuminated an enemy aircraft a patrolling Blenheim took too long to reach the scene and had difficulty in closing to attack. British hopes were centred on a later design from the same manufacturer, the Beaufighter, a derivative of the Beaufort torpedo bomber. This hardy twin-engine aircraft had four fixed 20mm cannon in the nose plus six .303s in the wings from which a single burst, fired by the pilot, could bring a 'kill'. The Beaufighter's top speed was in excess of 300mph, and it also possessed a good endurance. The type did not come into service until September 1940, when the first two of Fighter Command's seven Blenheim squadrons commenced conversion.

Aware of the Blenheim's shortcomings in the night fighter role, selected pilots in Hurricane and Spitfire squadrons attempted interceptions at night, usually during bright moon periods. The Spitfire, with its narrow-track undercarriage, was not easy to land in darkness and the type was soon withdrawn from this activity owing to several landing accidents. The Hurricane was the more suited type and individual freelance sorties in assigned patrols areas became a regular task. By No-

vember 1940 two Hurricane squadrons had become dedicated night fighter units and others were formed exclusively for this purpose. The Defiant was given a new lease of life, it being thought that the turret fighter might have an advantage in positioning below an enemy bomber, its target silhouetted in the night sky. In practice the Defiant was no more successful than other types in locating an enemy, whose most likely give-away was engine exhaust glow. Successful combats were few and far between, with only one aircraft brought down for, approximately, every 300 enemy sorties during the night raids of November and December 1940. In fact, through accident RAF night fighter losses during the same period were higher than those of the enemy they sought.

An obvious way to strike back at the night bomber, already employed with success by the *Luftwaffe*, was the despatch of fighters to the vicinity of enemy bases to catch the bombers as they prepared to land. In December 1940 Fighter Command assigned a squadron of Blenheims specifically to this duty, its first so-called intruder operation over France being flown on the night of the 21st. This activity was gradually increased with Hurricane, Defiant and Havoc units joining the Blenheims from early spring 1941. Initially contacts and claims were not numerous, but these sorties did cause a certain amount of disruption.

Intrusions into enemy territory were also being made by RAF day fighters. *Luftwaffe* activity over Britain in daylight was mostly confined to fighter-bomber raids and bad-weather sorties by single aircraft to give the defences little respite while

**Above:** The five swastikas on black-painted Defiant N1801/PS:Y indicate the victories of Flying Officer Fred Hughes and his gunner Sergeant Fred Gash. Three of the enemy aircraft were shot down at night (one with this machine), distinguishing the pair as one of the most accomplished in Defiants. Three new Defiant squadrons, formed for night fighting duties early in 1941, had but moderate success in finding targets. Hughes went on to be credited with another 13 and one shared while flying Beaufighters and Mosquitos, reaching the rank of Wing Commander. The Red Hand insignia on the nose of *Coimbatore II* denotes Hughes' Ulster background. After some nine months with No 264 at Colerne, N1801 became an instructional airframe. Note the 'flag' tied on the pitot tube as a 'don't damage me' warning. (IWM CH4810)

the main offensive was by night. The British realised that Hitler was unlikely to attempt a cross-Channel invasion during the winter, expecting the enterprise to be revived in the spring. To meet the threat Fighter Command was rapidly expanded, with new squadrons formed as quickly as equipment and personnel became available. Experienced pilots who had escaped from occupied Europe were gathered into squadrons named after their country of origin, a move which also helped maintain national pride. The total of Fighter Command squadrons had reached nearly 70 by the end of 1940, with more planned to be formed by the following spring. To prevent a build-up of shipping suitable for invasion purposes it was essential that the RAF kept up attacks on ports and harbours in northern France and the Low Countries.

A further measure to make invasion preparations difficult was constantly to harass the enemy air force, particularly his airfields that would be used during a renewed offensive. In similar fashion to *Luftwaffe* activities over southern England, a flight or pair of Hurricanes or Spitfires were sent out at low level to avoid radar detection, usually in poor weather where cloud could be used as cover, to strafe ground targets or attack any enemy aircraft encountered. This type of foray was known by the code-name 'Rhubarb' but, though frequently undertaken during the following two years, was usually little more than a painful nuisance to the enemy. More positive results were expected from bombing targets that did not entail deep penetration of enemy-held airspace and where substantial fighter escort could be provided. Such operations were usually referred to as 'Ramrods'. Other types of offensive action were 'Rodeos', which were squadron-strength fighter attacks on ground targets, while 'Roadsteads' were escorted attacks on shipping in harbour or at sea.

Despite the known performance advantages of the Me 109, the general RAF euphoria resulting from the exaggerated hurt inflicted on the *Jagdgruppen* in the summer of 1940 encouraged Fighter Command leaders to draw the enemy into combat in more positive ways. A device for achieving this was for formations of Blenheims, with substantial close escort and high cover, crossing in over the hostile coastline, arcing round and withdrawing. The presence of bombers was thought more likely to force the 'Emils' to oppose. Such a tactic had become known as a 'Circus'. On 10 January 1941 Circus No 1 was the first occasion since June that the RAF had despatched an escorted bomber force, the objective being an ammunition store in the Fôret de Guines. Six Blenheims with five squadrons of Hurricanes and six of Spitfires totalling 72 fighters were involved, and the *Luftwaffe* did respond. Against claims of two Me 109s brought down, one probably destroyed and two damaged, the British had a Hurricane shot down, another damaged and three badly shot-up Spitfires, one of which crashed while landing. In fact, no Me 109s were shot down.

Circus No 1 was the precursor to the whole cross-Channel offensive conducted by Fighter Command during the following two years, and was to some extent a reversal of the situation that existed for the *Luftwaffe* in the Battle of Britain—an exaggerated assessment of success through over-claiming. The losses incurred by Hurricane squadrons brought their more restricted use in these operations and Spitfires gradually became the predominant type sent to do battle. The Me 109 units were the more confident in dealing with British fighters in that they had now assumed the role of defenders and were aware that their enemy was intent on provoking combat. The general tactic that had proved so successful against their adversaries during the free-ranging sweeps of the previous summer were no longer hampered by the Messerschmitt's limited endurance. Now the dive from altitude, fire and break-away downward could be practised with the advantage of being able to choose a favourable situation to attack.

In an effort to redress the Me 109E's performance advantages, particularly at higher altitudes, a more powerful version of the Merlin engine had been a priority development. This appeared from production as the Merlin 45 in a new mark of Spitfire which was to become the most numerous production model, the Mk V. Apart from having a strengthened fuselage and embodying various refinements already introduced in production, the Spitfire V was simply a more powerful, cannon-armed version of the Mks I and II, although the eight .303 guns were retained on one version. In fact, a number of Mk I and II airframes were fitted with the new engine and brought up to Mk V standard from February 1941, with new production aircraft joining the squadrons in April. Unfortunately for Fighter Command, this coincided with the arrival of the Me 109F at *Luftwaffe* fighter bases in north-east France. Like the new Spitfire, the Messerschmitt had an upgraded powerplant but it also featured a redesigned wing with reduced loading, giving the model substantially better handling than the 'Emil'. This was achieved at the expense of a reduction in armament, none being carried in the wings. All weapons were fuselage-mounted, with a 20mm cannon firing through the propeller shaft and two rifle-calibre machine guns in the upper cowling of the engine, synchronised to fire through the propeller arc. This affirmed the *Luftwaffe*'s preference for fuselage-based armament rather than wing fixtures and the ranging problems associated with converging fire. Even with the arrival of the Me 109F, the RAF believed that the Spitfire V had a perform-

**Right:** In lieu of Beaufighters several Douglas Boston light bombers were modified to have a fixed nose gun installation of four (later eight) .303in machine guns for night work and were known as Havocs. No 23 Squadron received these to replace Blenheim IFs in March 1941. They intruded over *Luftwaffe* bomber bases in France and the Low Countries, where, attacking bombers as they left for or returned from raids over England, they achieved successes. The Havoc, not only much faster than the Blenheim, had better endurance. Losses were high but Havoc I BD121 had a charmed life and was eventually turned over to the Admiralty. (IWM CH2786)

**Right:** The Bristol Beaufighter. Photographed on 23 May 1941, Mk VIF X7920/BQ:F, in overall matt black finish, served with No 600 Squadron at Colerne. It was equipped with early AI radar, and after being withdrawn for modifications it was sent to No 96 Squadron and lost in a bad-weather flying accident, hitting trees near Wellsbourne Mountford on 7 November 1942. No 600 received its first Beaufighters in September 1940 as one of the first night fighter squadrons to convert from the Blenheim IF. In addition to being heavily armed, the Beaufighter, had a top speed of over 300mph and a relatively spacious interior to hold the bulky early radar equipment. (IWM CH17801)

ance advantage, but in reality the Messerschmitt still had the lead above 20,000ft.

The Hurricane II, first entering service in the autumn, also had a more powerful Merlin engine, the XX model, from which the Spitfire's Merlin 45 was developed. A twelve-gun version of the Hurricane II was available but during the spring of 1941 an all-cannon armament was preferred, the first Hurricane IIs with four 20mm weapons reaching the squadrons in April. Even with increased power it was plain that the Hurricane, fine aircraft that it was, could not be developed as a high-performance fighter. Much was expected from new Hawker designs, the Tornado and Typhoon, but their readying for production was beset with problems, particularly with the Vulture engine for the Tornado so that this design was discontinued. An even more laggardly introduction was that of the Westland Whirlwind. Difficulties with engines and armament continued to delay operational employment, and the first squadron was not equipped until December 1940. Although the Whirlwind had a good performance it was costly to produce. It was not judged worthy of further development, and Fighter Command put its faith in the Spitfire and the Typhoon.

Quantity was the overriding factor in preparing to meet a renewed *Luftwaffe* onslaught in the spring of 1941, and by June Fighter Command had double the strength of twelve months earlier. But the Command's immediate operational concern continued to be combating the night bomber. Airborne Interception radar was developing apace, each new model improving the range at which an aircraft could be detected and held. The system of vectoring the night fighter to a target bomber, known as Ground Control Interception (GCI), evolved with one site in each sector using radar tracking to feed the positions of aircraft to a control room, which in turn gave a night fighter crew radioed directions towards an enemy bomber. With technical improvements GCI could bring the night fighter to within a thousand yards of its quarry by the spring of 1941, and the latest AI radars enabled Beaufighter crews significantly to increase their combat successes. There was a comparative lull in *Luftwaffe* night bombing during February 1941, but the following month, when the nightly Blitz was again pursued in strength, AI night fighters for the first time took their claims into double figures.

During April the *Luftwaffe* flew more than 5,000 night sorties over Britain, including the heaviest raid of the Blitz when, on the 19th, some 700 enemy bombers attacked London, causing over 3,000 casualties. On this date 28 of the 48 destroyed claims by night fighters were AI contacts. Even so, overall during the winter and early spring more enemy aircraft had fallen to visual sightings by Hurricane pilots than to airborne radar-guided contacts, although the latter were on the way to becoming the most effective measure in dealing with the night bomber. In May 96 enemy aircraft destroyed were attributed to night fighter action and 41 to AA guns and balloons. This was approximately one for every 20 enemy sorties as against one for every 218 sorties the previous January. The night sky over Britain was becoming increasingly dangerous for the *Luftwaffe*. Then, in June 1941, its activities over Britain suddenly lessened: the *Kampfgruppen* were being withdrawn to support Hitler's eastern adventure against the Soviet Union.

# 6
# THE SOVIET SCENE

Despite Stalin's collusion with Hitler over the occupation of Poland, Britain was quick to accept the USSR as an ally in the struggle against the common enemy. War material was offered and accepted, fighter aircraft being an urgent requirement. Curtiss P-40B Tomahawks obtained from the United States were sent in one of the first sea convoys, these aircraft having been found wanting in performance in the fighter role and used for army cooperation, providing fast tactical reconnaissance and ground attack. There were still insufficient Spitfires for the RAF's own requirements, and the only type that could be spared was the Hurricane. Realising that the *Luftwaffe* would be given the task of bombing the convoys when they arrived in north-west Russia, it was agreed that an RAF contingent would be sent with Hurricane IIs to defend the ports against air attack. Subsequently the fighters would be turned over to Soviet pilots and the RAF men returned to Britain.

In July 1941 two squadrons were re-formed with Hurricanes and sent to the USSR on the carrier HMS *Argus* to Vaenga, near Murmansk. They became operational in September and were soon in action, making total claims of 20 enemy aircraft destroyed during the next six weeks, not without suffering losses, particularly when the ubiquitous Me 109 was encountered. After familiarising Soviet pilots and ground crews with the Hurricane, the squadrons' RAF personnel were withdrawn, the first at the end of October, the second a few weeks later. Many shipments of Hurricanes went to the USSR during the next few months, the eventual total of the type supplied being nearly 3,000, although some of the aircraft came via the Middle East.

The Hurricane had a decidedly better performance than any of the indigenous fighters serving with the Soviet forces in 1941. In time the Russians produced models that could match the German opposition, but for more than two years their successes came chiefly through force of numbers. A generally injudicious use of Soviet combat aircraft often provided the *Jagdgruppen* pilots with plentiful targets, particularly as many Russian pilots had little combat training. Many *Experten* appeared among the ranks of the *Jagdflieger*, the very talented running up extraordinary totals for enemy aircraft shot down. The USSR was a combat air front where the advantages of superior aircraft, tactics and training were patently obvious.

**Right:** A Hurricane IIB of No 81 Squadron reflected in the puddles left by early winter rains at Vaenga airfield near Murmansk. With No 134 Squadron, No 81 formed No 151 Wing, commanded by Wing Commander G. R. Isherwood. At this time, October 1941, RAF personnel were training Soviet pilots to fly and mechanics to service the Hurricanes, which explains the dual identification markings—numerals for the Russians and letter codes for the RAF. (IWM CR11)

# 7
# THE CROSS-CHANNEL CONTEST

With Britain having gained an ally in the east, there was even more incentive to maintain pressure in the west, and the only service able to take the war directly to the enemy was the RAF. Bomber Command was the obvious candidate, but Fighter Command was encouraged to pursue the cross-Channel forays.

Fighter Command had been under the command of Air Vice-Marshal Sholto Douglas since late November 1940, when the RAF hierarchy decided that Dowding should be moved on. Some senior officers found Dowding difficult and inflexible, which no doubt played a part in his relief. Air Vice-Marshal Park, who had ably guided No 11 Group through the Battle of Britain was replaced by Leigh-Mallory the following month, the latter's views on fighter control and tactics obviously having impressed the new Fighter Command leader. The offensive role which Fighter Command had developed during the first six months of 1941 was one which commended itself to Britain's Air Staff and government, besides which it was the RAF's creed to take the offensive—although in this case the true re-

sults of the cross-Channel ventures continued to be veiled by the inflated claims of the participants, particularly the British, who had no means of verification as the Me 109s shot down fell in occupied territory or in the sea.

Operating at high speed in hostile airspace became Standing Operational Procedure (SOP) for the RAF fighters, for anything less made then too vulnerable if 'bounced', RAF parlance for a surprise attack. Flying with an advanced throttle consumed fuel at an alarming rate and reduced endurance substantially, thus restricting operations to no more than 50 miles' penetration over land at the nearest point, the Pas de Calais.

The RAF then had the same problems that *Luftwaffe* fighters faced the previous year over south-east England, only more so. Not only had the Me 109Fs better high-altitude performance, allowing them to pursue the highly successful dive-and-run tactics; as there were no bombers to protect, the *Jagdgruppen* leaders could pick an opportune time to launch an attack. If the Spitfires were high the Me 109s would, whenever possible, be higher. Even when the Spitfires held the advan-

**Left:** To encourage national savings a scheme was devised whereby individuals or organisations could 'buy' an aircraft by contributing an amount equivalent to the cost. In the case of a Spitfire £5,000 was the figure and the 'presented' aircraft carried a suitable inscription in acknowledgement. *Observer Corps,* P7666/EB:Z, did its promoters well when used by No 41 Squadron's CO, Squadron Leader Donald Finlay: as his personal aircraft it was used to shoot down two Me 109Es in November 1940. Photographed at Hornchurch in December 1940, this Spitfire IIA was transferred to No 54 Squadron in the following February but shot up by an Me 109 on 24 April 1941 and abandoned. D. O. Finlay, a British Olympic hurdler, had been wounded in another Spitfire and forced to take to his parachute in August 1940. (IWM CH1888)

tage of height the Me 109 pilots knew that they were unlikely to be caught when diving to evade. The standard evasive manoeuvre of *Luftwaffe* fighters was what the British pilots termed the 'split S', a half roll and dive away under. The main defensive move for British fighters, if an enemy attack was seen in time, was to execute a sharp turn to face him. If effected neither side was in much danger from a head-on pass. Generally, endurance confined RAF raids to a set pattern which the enemy could anticipate and meet with advantage. To some extent individual RAF squadrons still chose their own formations and tactics. Many continued using the vulnerable three-plane flights and string formations while others had appreciated the *Luftwaffe*'s dual pair from which a 'finger four' eventually came to be the standard flight formation.

So confident was the *Luftwaffe* of dealing with RAF daylight intrusions that, following the attack on Russia, only three *Jagdgeschwader* were left in the west, one in the general Brittany area, another in the Pas de Calais and the third in the Netherlands/north-west Germany. The number of fighters fluctuated between 200 and 300 as *Jagdgruppen* were withdrawn and replaced. The strongest forces were usually placed between Rouen and Antwerp, which was the main area of RAF day

**Above:** Pilots of No 257 Squadron getting into parachute harness prior to a flight from Coltishall in January 1941. The parachute pack acted as the seat cushion and also proved to be an excellent buffer, preventing cannon shell splinters ending up in a pilot's rear end. The Hurricane is Squadron Leader 'Bob' Stanford Tuck's, in which he made several claims; his scoreboard of swastikas is painted on the side of the cockpit. Pilot Officer Gerald North also shot down an enemy aircraft using V6864/DT:A when the CO was on leave. This was a Fiat BR.20 during the famous Italian raid of 11 November 1940. The Hurricane was eventually retired to No 56 OTU and crashed at Walpole St Andrew, Norfolk—the pilot being killed—after colliding with a Manchester on 24 November 1941. (IWM CH1926)

fighter activity. The limited range of the British fighters greatly aided the effective deployment of the *Luftwaffe*'s units.

The experience of the early daylight offensive operations had caused the Air Staff to opine that the long-range fighter could not compete with the short-range interceptor. In May 1941 Prime Minister Winston Churchill had wanted to know what could be done about increasing the range of British fighters. In his reply, dated 27 May, Air Chief Marshal Portal, Chief of the Air Staff, concluded by stating, 'Increased range can only be provided at the expense of performance and manoeuvrability. The long-range fighter, whether built specifically as such, or whether given increased range by fitting extra tanks, will be at a disadvantage compared with the short-range, high-performance fighter. All our experience to date confirms this . . .' Churchill was not convinced and responded, 'We have got to adapt machines to the distances which have to be traversed . . . we ought to attempt daylight raids into Germany for bombing on a severe scale. If this is not done, you will be helpless in the West and beaten in the East.'

It is clear from the foregoing and other exchanges that at this time the RAF, like the *Luftwaffe*, saw the long-range fighter as necessitating a twin-engine machine, and one thus unable to compete with the smaller, agile, single-engine types. Moreover, with Bomber Command mainly commited to night operations, there was no need for a long-range escort fighter. The irony of the situation was that an aircraft with the potential the Air Ministry declared unachievable had been designed and was already in production for the RAF in the United States.

The Circuses, Rodeos, Ramrods, Roadsteads and Rhubarbs continued apace, and while there was no lack of confidence in tackling the enemy at squadron level, tests with a captured Me 109F brought a more sobering view of the situation in RAF technical circles—even more so when a new radial-engine German fighter was encountered in July 1941. At first met only occasionally, the Focke Wulf Fw 190A became fully op-

**Below:** Flight Lieutenant Charles B. F. Kingcome in the cockpit of his Spitfire, QJ:F, at Manston on 6 February 1941. His squadron, No 92, claimed to be the top-scorer in the battles of 1940 with 127 enemy aircraft shot down and 60 probables, although later evaluation suggests the true figure was in the region of 80 destroyed. The squadron was sent to Egypt early in 1942 and was without Spitfires for some months, but still claimed to be the top-scoring RAF fighter squadron of the war with 317 victories. Kingcome claimed nine enemy aircraft during his time with No 92 despite being shot down himself and spending some time in hospital recovering from wounds. (IWM CH17308)
**Right:** The much-needed cannon armament came with production Spitfire VBs plus many Mk I and II models transformed into Mk Vs. R6923 (shown) started operational life as a Mk I, having a cannon wing fitted in July 1940 for the first operational tests by No 19 Squadron. In April 1941 it was returned to Rolls-Royce and had a Merlin 45 installed and went to No 92 Squadron at Biggin Hill, from where it was flown for a photographic session on 19 May by Flight Lieutenant Allan

Wright, who claimed R6923 as his fourth QJ:S. With Sergeant G. W. Ashton the aircraft failed to return from a sweep on 21 June 1941, another victim of the Me 109F. The 'bumps' in the upper surfaces of the wings covered the 60-round drum for the Hispano 20mm cannon. The weapon had a length of $51\frac{1}{2}$in, and it was necessary for most of the barrel to extend beyond the wing leading edge, where it was encased in a recoil shroud. The muzzle velocity of these weapons was 2,885ft/sec. Allan Wright destroyed eleven enemy aircraft and shared three with other pilots before being removed from operational flying. (IWM CH2929)

**Left, upper:** Pilot Officer Eric Lock of No 611 Squadron in Spitfire VB W3247/FY:Z on return to Hornchurch from a sweep, 6 July 1941. Lock flew with No 41 Squadron during the Battle of Britain, claiming more than 20 enemy aircraft. He was badly wounded in the limbs by cannon shell splinters when shot up by an Me 109 on 17 November 1940. Although managing to crash-land his Spitfire near Martlesham Heath, he was too badly injured to leave the cockpit and nearly two hours elapsed before he was found by two soldiers who carried him the two miles to the station on an improvised stretcher of rifles and greatcoats. After a long period in hospital and convalescence he was posted to No 611 Squadron. On 3 August 1941 he failed to return from strafing German troops and is presumed to have been shot down and killed by ground fire. (IWM CH3057)

**Left, lower:** To acknowledge United States support for Britain, the Air Ministry established three fighter squadrons for American volunteers. The first of these 'Eagle Squadrons' was No 71, formed in September 1940 to fly Brewster Buffalos. These tubby American fighters were soon replaced by Hurricanes, with which the squadron became operational in February 1941. Two of the original 'characters' were Chesley Peterson and Gregory Daymond, the former being the only pilot in the squadron who had US Army Air Corps flying training; Gus Daymond had obtained piloting experience with commercial enterprises. Both had good fortune in air fighting and both eventually rose to command the squadron. At the time this photograph was taken, at North Weald on 10 October 1941, 23-year-old Flight Lieutenant Peterson had claims for two air victories and four probables in 42 sorties. Flying Officer Daymond (in cockpit) at 21 the youngest member of No 71, had five victories in 27 sorties. (IWM CH3736)

**Right:** To meet the wave-hopping, hit-and-run *Luftwaffe* raiders, a Chain Home Low radar network was set up round the east and south coast of England in 1941. This is the station at Hopton, Suffolk. (IWM CH15183)

erational in September and gradually the two *Jagdgeschwader* based in France were re-equipped with the type. The Fw 190, like most new types, suffered its technical problems, particularly with the engine, but it soon proved to be the complete master of the Spitfire V. Despite their claims—and many Fw 190s were shot down by Spitfire Vs—it was very obvious to Fighter Command pilots that they now faced a far more formidable opponent than the Me 109F. Indeed, in November 1941 day operations over north-west Europe were more restricted as a result. The true picture of the air fighting during 1941 was

the loss of two and a half RAF fighters for every one of the enemy's.

While part of Fighter Command's predicament was a result of the German aviation industry's encouragement during pre-war years which gave a technical lead, the development of new and improved fighters and engines in Britain had been somewhat tardy. Much was expected of the Hawker Typhoon, which began to reach the squadrons in September 1941 only to disappoint. Not only was it beset with continuing technical problems, particularly related to the powerful Napier Sabre engine, but its performance other than at low level was disappointing. In fact, when an Fw 190 pilot mistakenly landed on an English airfield and he and his machine were captured, the RAF had an opportunity to compare performances with its own fighters and concluded that the Typhoon had little to commend it for fighter-versus-fighter combat. The crisis over fighter performance brought demands for the advanced Spitfire VIII, which made use of a more powerful version of the Merlin engine incorporating a two-stage mechanical supercharger. Not wanting to await Mk VIII production, a stop-gap was requested, the installation of the Merlin 61 engine in a Mk V airframe resulting

**Above:** The Focke-Wulf Fw 190A had a better all-round performance than the Spitfire V. It was faster in level flight, climb and dive. The rate of roll was exceptional and only in turning ability was the Spitfire superior in manoeuvres. The sheer nature of air fighting saw many Focke-Wulfs shot down by Spitfire Vs, but the combat ratio was somewhere between two and three Spitfires for every Fw 190 shot down. (Bruce Robertson collection)

**Left:** Nos 56 and 242 Squadrons set out from North Weald on a fighter sweep in June 1941, still adhering to the three-plane section with a solitary weaver to guard the rear. It would be some months before the RAF universally employed and developed the four-plane, two-element section, similar to that used by the *Luftwaffe* fighters. (IWM CH3780)

**Right, upper:** On 28 September 1941 Squadron Leader Arthur E. Donaldson DFC AFC was leading No 263 Squadron Whirlwinds in attacking Morlaix airfield when his aircraft, P7044, was hit in three places by ground fire. A 20mm shell shattered the cockpit hood and glanced his helmet, sufficiently hard enough to render him momentarily unconscious. Despite a very sore head and slight wounds in both arms, he brought the Whirlwind safely back to Predannack. In a subsequent tour in Malta as a flying Wing Commander he was severely wounded, losing two fingers. Two of his brothers also served as RAF fighter pilots: Squadron Leader John W. Donaldson, who had commanded No 263 Squadron in Norway and was lost when HMS *Glorious* was sunk; and Teddy Donaldson, a 1940 Hurricane pilot, who as a Group Captain achieved a world speed record of 610mph in 1946. (IWM CH9618)

in the Spitfire IX. Comparison tests showed that not only was the Mk IX a match for the Fw 190A below 20,000ft, it was much superior at higher altitudes and well able to deal with the Me 109F. However, the Me 109G, becoming operational in May 1942 boasted a larger engine with an emergency facility for nitrous oxide injection, giving short boost speeds in excess of 400mph. The 'Gustav', although very similar to the 'Friedrich' in appearance, was heavier, and in some respects its performance and handling were inferior, albeit not excessively. The new model was first used for providing a high-altitude element in each French-based *Jagdgeschwader* to meet the Fw 190's deficiency in this area.

Spitfire IXs went into squadron service in June 1942 but the lack of Merlin 61 engines made re-equipment of the host of Mk V units extremely slow. By August Fighter Command had four squadrons with the new mark, all in No 11 Group, and such was the shortage that, for many months thereafter, when squadrons were withdrawn to another group the Spitfires IXs were left behind for use by the replacement squadrons. While for the first time some of their number had an interceptor fighter that was a fair match for the opposition, the majority of Fighter Command squadrons soldiered on with the Spitfire V and frequently found themselves outfought.

The United States entered the war in December 1941 and with a 'beat Germany first' policy was intent on establishing a

**Right:** Eire may have been officially neutral during the Second World War but many of its nationals volunteered to fight in the British services. One of the most famous was Brendan E. Finucane, a Dubliner. He shot down at least five enemy aircraft while with No 65 Squadron from August 1940 to April 1941. He then went to No 452, which was forming as the first Australian-manned squadron in Britain, with whom he added another eighteen victories, all Me 109s and including sorties which brought four 'doubles' and a 'triple'. This photograph was taken at Kenley on 13 October 1941, on which day Finucane (centre) claimed two Me 109Fs during a sweep over the Pas de Calais, three days before his 21st birthday. In January 1942, given command of No 602 Squadron, he continued to have several successful combats, and by June, when promoted to Wing Commander to lead the Hornchurch Wing, he had 29 victories and several probables. His luck ran out on 15 July: when he was crossing out over the French coast at low altitude the engine of his Spitfire was hit by ground fire. Too low to bale out, Finucane unsuccessfully attempted to ditch the aircraft which went under as soon as it hit. This remarkable pilot was not seen again. (IWM CH3753)

substantial air force in Britain. In May and June 1942 the first two USAAF fighter groups to arrive in England were equipped with Spitfire Vs, their Bell P-39 Airacobras flown in the United States being deemed unsuitable fighters for operations in Europe. The three squadrons of one group, operating under Fighter Command, joined 58 RAF fighter squadrons in the Dieppe enterprise of 19 April 1942. This seaborne raid involving Canadian troops was highly costly in lives and equipment, not least in the air where force of numbers successfully shielded the ground and sea operations. The Allies lost 106 aircraft, of which 88 were fighters; the *Luftwaffe* lost 48, of which 23 were fighters, although a total 92 of all types were claimed by Allied air crews.

The cross-Channel operations of 1942 cost RAF Fighter Command 587 fighters and the *Luftwaffe* 198, nearly one for every three. Faced with increasing activity, the *Luftwaffe* built up its fighter strength in western Europe to over 450 by the end of 1942, in part due to the daylight intrusions of American heavy bombers at an optimum 25,000ft. A new phase in the fighter-versus-fighter conflict was about to begin.

**Left, upper:** A squadron line-up such as these Spitfire VBs of No 92 at Digby on 2 December 1941 was usually only considered wise if far away from south-east England and hit-and-run Messerschmitts. The nearest aircraft, W3444/QJ:F, *New Yorklin*, is that of the CO, Squadron Leader Richard Milne DFC, and has his scoreboard with eleven victory symbols below the cockpit. It was Fighter Command policy periodically to withdraw squadrons from offensive operations in the south to defensive duties further west or north in Britain, thus giving an opportunity for recuperation and retraining. In fact No 92 Squadron was about to be sent overseas to the Middle East, once there having to wait six months before Spitfires arrived. 'Dickie' Milne did not go overseas, being given another Fighter Command posting. Promoted to Wing Commander, early in 1943 he became Wing Leader at Biggin Hill. In this capacity he was leading the wing's Spitfire IXs on an operation over Belgium when they were bounced by Fw 190s. Having to bale out into the sea, Milne was rescued by the Germans to spend the rest of the war as a POW. (IWM CH4159)

**Left, lower:** German soldiers examine Spitfire V AA837/SD:E of No 501 Squadron, whose pilot, Pilot Officer E. H. Shore made a crash-landing on a Normandy beach owing to loss of coolant during a fighter sweep on 4 November 1941. (IWM HU65214)

**Right, upper:** Not the usual sort of sweep associated with RAF Fighter Command, but the station chimneys at Kirton-in-Lindsey had to be cleared. Pushing his bicycle along the edge of the hangar apron, the local sweep passes Spitfire IIA P8657 of No 121 Squadron, the second Eagle Squadron formed with American volunteers. The squadron had just completed its working-up period and re-equipment with Spitfire VBs (one of which can be seen in the background) before moving south for cross-Channel operations a few days after this photograph was taken in late November 1941. P8657,

presentation aircraft *City of Leicester III*, served with five squadrons and two OTUs, finally becoming an instructional airframe in 1943. (S. Clay Collection)

**Right:** During 1941 46 new RAF fighter squadrons were formed in Britain, the usual procedure being to use combat-exposed pilots to fill the command positions and work up the squadron to combat proficiency at a station in Nos 12 or 13 Group. No 122 Squadron, to be associated with Bombay from funds presented, was formed at Turnhouse in May and stayed in the north until the following spring, much of the time at Scorton. Flight Lieutenant H. J. L. Hallowes, who had been credited with destroying 19 *Luftwaffe* aircraft in 1940 while flying Hurricanes with No 43 Squadron, was assigned as Flight Commander in December 1941 (when this photograph was taken) to impart his experience. 'Darkie' Hallowes, who had joined the RAF as a 16-year-old Halton apprentice in 1929, spent most of his war with Fighter Command, serving with six different squadrons and eventually making Wing Commander. The Spitfire V is BM252/MT:E. (IWM CH4275)

**Above:** The squadrons using Hurricanes for fighter-bombing often referred to their aircraft as 'Hurribombers'. The usual load for cross-Channel operations was a 250lb HE bomb on each wing rack. The first squadron to train for this work was No 402, the second RCAF fighter squadron formed in Britain. It flew its first fighter-bomber raid with eight so-called 'Hurribombers' on 1 November 1941, an attack on a *Luftwaffe* airfield at Berck-sur-Mer. BE485/AE:W, one of the aircraft involved, is seen here with two 250lb HE bombs during a demonstration flight, flown by Flight Sergeant Keene from No 402's base at Warmwell on 6 January 1942. (IWM CH4567)

**Left:** The early Spitfire's endurance was limited to around an hour at cruise speed. To extend this, auxiliary fuel tanks were installed. An early type was a 70 Imp gallon installation on the left wing. This was confined to those Spitfire units operating in areas where *Luftwaffe* interceptors would be unlikely to be encountered, in particular coastal shipping protection patrols. No 152 Squadron operated with these wing tanks on Spitfire IIAs for convoy protection in the winter of 1941/42. The photograph, taken on 22 December 1941 at Coltishall, shows the squadron CO, Squadron Leader John Darwen, in *Guntur III* (believed P7448), and Flight Lieutenant P. F. Illingsworth, in *Gibraltar* (P8394), taxying out for take-off to fly to Portreath. (IWM CH4383)

**Right, upper:** The display of 29 swastikas on the side of this Spitfire VB, RS:T, indicates the record of Wing Commander Robert Stanford Tuck, the Wing Leader at Biggin Hill in January 1942. One of the most colourful RAF pilots of the Battle of Britain, 'Bob' Stanford Tuck had to 'belly' his Spitfire in on the 28th of that month when it was hit by ground fire while on a strafing sortie. Captured, before being sent to a POW camp Tuck was entertained by Adolf Galland at *JG 26*'s base. After the war Tuck and Galland became good friends. (S. Clay Collection)

**Right, lower:** The RAF formed twelve fighter squadrons manned largely by Polish nationals. The most renowned pilot was Stanislaw Skalski, right, seen here at Church Stanton in the spring of 1942 with Tadeus Czerwinski embracing their national emblem. At the time both were Flight Lieutenants and Flight Leaders, Czerwinski being promoted to Squadron Leader and given command of No 306 Squadron in April that year, only to be shot down and killed by ground fire near St Omer in August. Skalski was born 1915 in Russia of Polish parents. He joined the Polish Air Force in 1936 and when flying PZL P.11 fighters claimed six *Luftwaffe* aircraft during the September 1939 *Wehrmacht* offensive. Eventually finding his way to Britain and the first of the RAF Polish squadrons then training, through his impatience to see action he was transferred to No 501 Squadron at Kenley, with whom he shot down seven enemy aircraft in as many days. Further success was obtained with No 306 and No 316 Squadrons during the next year and in the spring of 1943 with the special Spitfire IX flight he took to North Africa. As a Wing Commander he led a Mustang III wing in 1944 before being confined to staff appointments. With 22 1/4 accredited victories, he was the most successful of all the Polish pilots. On return to Poland he was imprisoned by the Communists for nearly eight years, although thereafter he was permitted so serve in their air force, retiring as a General. (IWM CH4793)

**Left:** Squadron Leader Keith W. Truscott, a redhead, joined No 452 Squadron as a Pilot Officer in the summer of 1941 and rose to command the unit within eight months. During this time he had been credited with 11 victories, all Me 109s. Here, photographed at Redhill on 12 March 1942, 'Bluey' Truscott stands before his Spitfire VB AB994, *Gingerbread,* with which he shot down two more enemy aircraft in March 1942, one an Fw 190. Later the same month, when his squadron was sent to Australia, he also returned to his homeland. Keith Truscott lost his life in a non-combat accident the following year. *Gingerbread,* 'presented' by red-headed Australian women, was lost with No 457 Squadron on 4 April 1942. (IWM CH5114)

**Right:** A Spitfire VB of No 457 Squadron comes into land at Redhill, March 1942. This RAAF-manned squadron had but two months' operational activity in an offensive role before being sent off to northern Australia for the defence of Darwin. Its CO during this period was Squadron Leader Peter M. Brothers, a distinguished Battle of Britain Hurricane pilot who made No 457's first claim on 26 March 1942. (IWM CH5249)

**Below:** The Air Fighting Development Unit was set up specially to devise and test equipment and tactics using a variety of aircraft types. Occasionally participating in operations, it had both losses and claims in air fighting. Spitfire I P7290 has an ice guard on the carburettor air intake and a towing hook aft of the tailwheel. This fighter, serving with No 611 Squadron, had been damaged by return fire from a Do 17 which Flying Officer Douglas Watkins shot down near Skegness on 21 August 1940. After six months with the AFDU at Duxford it was eventually turned over to the Royal Navy. (IWM CH5291)

**Left:** If one lived long enough promotion could come rapidly. Flight Sergeant William Loud joined No 602 Squadron early in 1942, obtained a commission and was a Flight Lieutenant before leaving No 602 in the summer of 1943. The following year, as a Squadron Leader, he was given No 19 Squadron and within three months was promoted Wing Commander to lead a Mustang wing. Photographed at Redhill on 21 May 1942, Bill Loud is about to leave BM124/LO:W, *Queen Salote*, presented by the Queen of Tonga. At the time this Spitfire VB, which came to No 602 on 1 April 1942, had sustained nine battle repairs during 51 operational sorties. Pilots flying this aircraft claimed two enemy fighters destroyed as well as a probable and three damaged. It endured throughout hostilities, serving with seven different squadrons before being struck off charge in 1946. IWM CH5575.

**Below:** While a ground staff man holds his parachute, Squadron Leader Michael G. F. Pedley prepares to board Spitfire VB BM420/NX:A at Tangmere, 8 June 1942. At this time the revised fuselage roundels and fin flashes were being introduced, and this aircraft was the first in the squadron to have the narrow yellow and white rings. CO of No 131 Squadron during its introduction to offensive operations, Pedley was promoted to Wing Commander after finishing his tour and detailed to command a fighter wing destined for the North African invasion. In the Mediterranean war zone he became famous for being a man of 'firsts': he was the first British pilot to land in Algeria on the day of the invasion, the first to land at Athens after the German withdrawal in October 1944, and the first into Crete the following month. Although by then a Group Captain, he frequently participated in combat operations which, following the dearth of enemy aircraft in the area, generally involved ground attack on a wide variety of targets. BM420 *Spirit of Kent* had a double life in that it was later rebuilt as a Seafire I for the Royal Navy and given a new serial, NX923. (IWM CH5883)

**Above:** New shapes in the sky: Typhoon IAs of No 56 Squadron in a 'finger four' section over Duxford, June 1942. No 56 was the first squadron to receive this big Hawker fighter and they had abandoned the old three-plane flight by this time. (IWM CH9256)

**Right:** There can have been few more imposing names in RAF Fighter Command than that of Flight Lieutenant the Count Yvan Georges Arsene Felician du Monceau de Bergendael; he is seen here on 22 July 1942 at Kenley with his personal Spitfire VB *Usoke*, EN794, of No 350 Squadron, the largely Belgian-manned unit of Fighter Command. More generally referred to in the RAF as Ivan du Monceau, this officer had a tour with No 609 Squadron, with which unit the five victories recorded on his aircraft were obtained. The small square with four helmets apparently applies to strafing enemy troops. Promoted to Squadron Leader, Count du Monceau commanded No 349 (Belgian) Squadron on formation in January 1943. He proved the most successful Belgian pilot in air combat with eight confirmed, three probable and six damaged credits. (IWM CH6352)

*The Fight for the Skies*

**Left:** Jockey caps and fatigues to the fore: Eglinton, Northern Ireland, early August 1942. USAAF mechanics of the 52nd Fighter Group prepare to aid starting RAF Spitfire VB EB:K, inherited from the RAF's No 41 Squadron. Ground crews for the first Spitfire-equipped American units were trained at RAF establishments. (S. Clay Collection)

**Below left:** Air support for the ill-conceived Dieppe raid of 19 August 1942 cost 80 RAF and eight USAAF Spitfires, most through diving attacks from *Luftwaffe* fighters flying at higher altitudes. No 111 Squadron was comparatively fortunate, losing but two aircraft, one to flak. The CO, Squadron Leader Peter R. Wickham DFC, made claims of two Fw 190s damaged during the five sorties he flew this day in Spitfire VB EP166/JU:N, two while leading the newcomer USAAF 308th Fighter

Squadron. Photographed here at Kenley five days later, Wickham went on to be credited with ten enemy aircraft shot down, seven probables and fifteen damaged by the end of hostilities. His first successful combat was made with a No 33 Squadron Gladiator in Libya in January 1940 and his last was against an Fw190 off the Norwegian coast flying a Mustang IV of the Peterhead Wing in March 1945. His service with various units included a few weeks in summer 1944 with the USAAF 4th Fighter Group P-51s. *O Bandeirante,* 'presented' by São Paulo, Brazil, was rebuilt as a Seafire IB in June 1943. (IWM CH6826)

**Above:** Spitfire VB EN799/MX:R of the 307th Fighter Squadron taxies out for take off at Westhampnet, 28 August 1942. The occasion was a sweep which proved uneventful. A unit of the 31st Fighter Group, the

307th was the first USAAF fighter organisation to become operational in the ETO. (USAAF)

**Below:** With four 20mm Oerlikon cannon the Hurricane IIC had considerable firepower but its performance was such that RAF Fighter Command was loath to commit the type against Me 109Fs or Fw 190As in cross-Channel sweeps. No 3 Squadron, based at Hunsdon, went over to night fighting duties at around the time this photograph of BD867/QO:Y was taken. The aircraft has a flash guard fitted to the fuselage to help shield the pilot's eyes from exhuast glow. BD867 was lost in the Channel with Sergeant S. D. Banks RCAF while engaged in attacking gun emplacements during the notorious Dieppe raid of 19 August 1942. (IWM CH3504)

**Above:** The appearance of sub-stratosphere raiders over Britain led to the development of a high-altitude version of the Spitfire, the Mk VI, of which there was only limited production, 97 serving in special flights in eight squadrons. Based on a Mk V airframe fitted with a pressurised cockpit, a high-altitude-rated Merlin 47 engine and extended wing-tips, the Spitfire VI could operate comfortably at 40,000ft. Part of the air intake for the pressuring system can be seen below the exhaust stack on BR579/ON:H of No 124 Squadron at North Weald on 24 November 1942. (IWM 18082).

**Left:** The CO of No 504 Squadron, Squadron Leader R. Lewis, comes into land at Middle Wallop in Spitfire VB EE624/TM:R in December 1942. Apart from an eight-day commitment during the Battle of France in 1940, the County of Nottingham Squadron was based in Britain throughout hostilities. A score of RAF Fighter Command squadrons were moved from Britain to the 'Torch' enterprise late in 1942 and many others were transferred to the 2nd Tactical Air Force and moved to the Continent following the launch of 'Overlord' in 1944. (IWM CH8015)

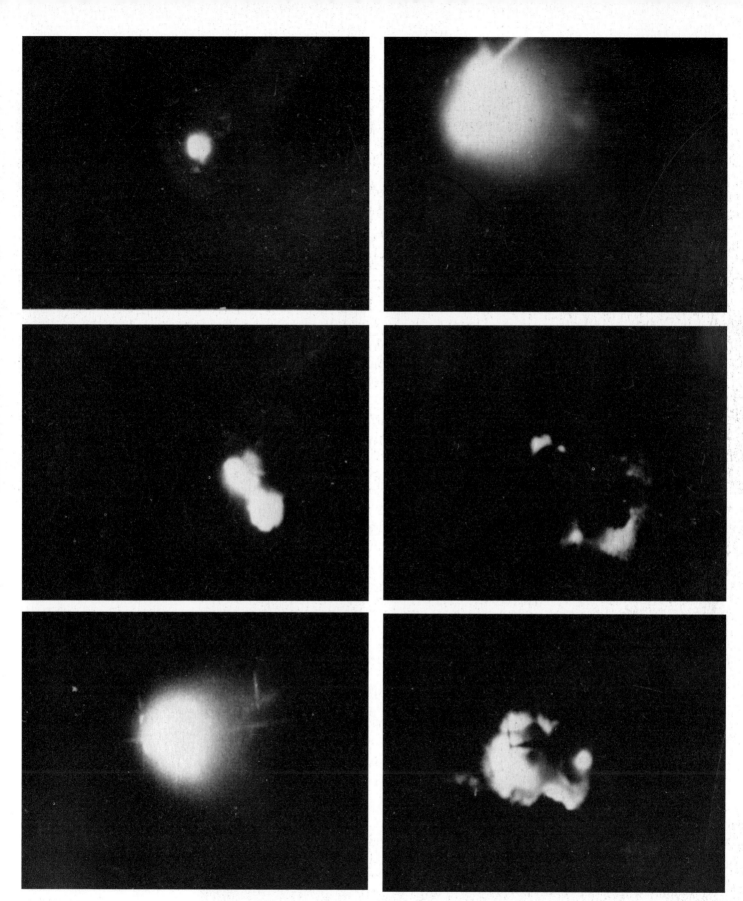

**Above:** Evidence of the vast improvement in effecting night interceptions is well illustrated by the fact that a single Beaufighter crew was credited with bringing down three Do 217 bombers on the night of 31 October/1 November 1942 over the south coast. This gun camera photograph shows the third victim under attack by Beaufighter IF V8233 near Foreness. This was the No 29 Squadron crew's sixth claim, but tragically Flying Officer George Pepper, 26, pilot, and Pilot Officer Joe Toone, 34, radar navigator, were killed making a test flight in another Beaufighter during daylight sixteen days later. The aircraft was seen to dive out of cloud into a field near Detling. (IWM C3262)

**Above:** Servicing Wing Commander Rupert F. H. Clerke's Beaufighter V8751 *Heart's Content* of No 125 (Newfoundland) Squadron at Fairwood Common on 2 January 1943. The approved Wing Commander's pennant is painted just forward of the inscription. Clerke used this aircraft to shoot down two enemy night raiders during 1943. (IWM CH8340)

**Left:** The Merchant Ship Fighter Unit was formed with volunteer pilots who flew Hurricanes catapulted from merchant vessels to intercept long-range *Luftwaffe* bombers. After dealing with the enemy the Hurricanes were abandoned by the pilots, who parachuted into the sea to be rescued, it was hoped, by the Royal Navy. Several interceptions were successful but Hurricane V6756/NJ:L was one aircraft never catapulted in anger. When photographed on 9 October 1941 at Greenock, it was being demonstrated from the SS *Empire Tide*. The launch rails were 75ft long and the launch cradle was propelled by thirteen electrically fired, solid-fuel rockets, accelerating the Hurricane to some 80mph. (IWM A9419)

# 8
# MIDDLE EAST FORTITUDE

On the outbreak of war the RAF had just two fighter squadrons in the area centred on Egypt and known as the Middle East. Both were equipped with Gloster Gladiators and their deployment was connected with the defence of the Suez Canal, a vital link in Britain's communications with the Empire. The serious situation in western Europe precluded reinforcement with modern fighters: it was not until June 1940 that a single Hurricane was added to the strength of one squadron and used for the first successful combat with an Italian aircraft soon after Mussolini took his country to war with Britain. Fortunately for the RAF the *Regia Aeronautica* was generally ill-trained and poorly equipped and led, if numerically stronger. True, the Savoia-Marchetti SM.79 medium bomber was nearly as fast as the Gladiator and the Fiat CR.42 biplane fighter its par. At this time the *Regia Aeronautica* had some 300 aircraft of all types in Libya and slightly more in East Africa, compared with the RAF's 200-odd in the Egypt area and 160 in British colonies and protectorates to the south-east.

More Hurricanes were soon forthcoming for a newly formed squadron and to convert one of the Gladiator units, enabling the RAF to achieve air superiority and aid the first desert land offensive which drove the Italians back to Benghazi by February 1941. Meanwhile a few Hurricanes had also been supplied to the squadrons, mainly South African Air Force (SAAF), fighting in East Africa to aid the successful completion of ground offensives which eliminated Italian forces in that area. Support of Greece, when that country was attacked by Italian forces from Albania, brought, in November, a Gladiator squadron from the Middle East, which began to receive Hurricanes two months later. Reinforcement with two squadrons from the Libyan campaign followed in February, one with Hurricanes the other with Gladiators. Here again there was no doubt about the superiority of the Hurricane over the opposition until the *Luftwaffe* appeared on the scene in April; then the small RAF contingent was soon overwhelmed by stronger opposition, which included Me 109s. Nevertheless, it was during the air fighting in Greece that, where numbers are the yardstick, the RAF's most successful fighter pilot of the war excelled. Squadron Leader Marmaduke Pattle is believed to have shot down at least 45 enemy aircraft before losing his life during an engage-

**Right:** A Gloster Gladiator takes off from an airfield in Egypt. With a top speed of around 250mph and armed with four rifle-calibre machine guns (two can be seen under the lower plane), this aircraft was outdated as a front-line fighter by 1939. Even so, it was used to good effect against the Italian Air Force during the first few months of hostilities in the Middle East. (IWM ME519A)

ment with Me 110s over Piraeus harbour on 20 April. The remnants of these RAF fighter squadrons withdrew to Crete and then to Palestine and the Middle East to re-form.

The Germans, having come to the aid of their ally, identified Malta as an immediate objective for elimination, the island being the base from which many air and sea attacks on supply shipping to Axis forces in North Africa were launched. Beginning in January 1941, frequent bombings were carried out, a small number of Me 109s flying from Sicily to deal with Malta's Hurricane squadron. A military force under General Erwin Rommel was sent to Tripolitania to reverse the fortunes of the Italian Army and in February the British were driven back, not least by the superior equipment of the German Army. A *Gruppe* of Me 109Es arrived in Libya in April and once again the RAF found itself having to operate Hurricanes at a disadvantage. Tomahawks, the RAF name for the Curtiss P-40B, brought into service during the summer, offered no improvement on the Hurricane in air combat, although it showed itself to be a hardy airframe in the desert environment. With a build-up of forces by both sides, in September a second *Luftwaffe Jagdgruppe* was sent to Africa, this one equipped with Me 109Fs, the other *Gruppe* converting to the model in December. Despite this the RAF had air superiority through strength of numbers, which were substantially increased during the summer.

By the late autumn there were over a thousand aircraft on hand with 280 fighter types in squadron service, three of these units being South African Air Force and one Royal Australian Air Force (RAAF). Nine of these squadrons had various marks of Hurricane and the remaining five Tomahawks. The losses suffered by these fighter squadrons were greater than those of the *Luftwaffe*, many being caused by operating at low level and thus being prone to 'bounces' from above. Even so, RAF bomber operations against enemy ground forces were rarely turned back, the Me 109 pilots tending to practise the fruitful tactics of flying up-sun and diving on opportune targets, usually fighters on the periphery the RAF strike forces, for, although the Hurricanes and Tomahawks averaged a two-to-one loss in combat with the Me 109s, they usually managed to shield the bombers.

A new British offensive put the *Afrika Korps* into retreat in December 1941 and back past Benghazi. Here extended supply lines forced the British to re-group, allowing Rommel to receive reinforcements. The thorn in his side continued to be Malta, and in the same month a new and heavier air campaign was launched against the beleaguered island. It was bombed both day and night, a concentrated effort beginning in late March. More than 4,000 *Luftwaffe* bomber sorties were flown against Malta in April, with as many fighter sorties in support. But, during March, Malta had received its first Spitfire Vs, flown off the carrier HMS *Eagle*; similar deliveries followed

during the next two months. As against Britain in 1940, the assault was intended to gain air superiority as a precondition to invasion, and, not dissimilarly, the inability to bring about this state delayed and finally saw the abandonment of invasion plans. Nevertheless, two-thirds of the Spitfires delivered during the summer of 1942 were lost to combat, bombing and accident within six months. Air Vice-Marshal Park, who had conducted operations for No 11 Group during the Battle of Britain, took command of the RAF in Malta during this period. When obtaining good advance warning from radar, he countered many of the daylight attacks by putting strong formations of fighters into the air to break up the enemy bombers by mass attack before they reached the island.

Meanwhile Rommel renewed the to-and-fro contest through Libya in February 1942. Once more the British soldier found himself fighting against superior equipment, notably armour, and was again forced into retreat, which was not halted until El Alamein in Egypt. Throughout the *Wehrmacht*'s advance the British again retained air superiority through strength of numbers. Rommel's advancing forces were continually harassed from the air, with Hurricane and Tomahawk squadrons engaged in ground attack, making them vulnerable to the Me 109s. During the spring and summer of 1942 one Me 109F pilot, *Leutnant* Hans-Joachim Marseille, ran up a score of 158 Allied aircraft shot down, mostly Hurricanes and Tomahawks, before being killed in a flying accident in September. *Jagdgruppe* attentions to the escorted Baltimore, Maryland and Boston bomber formations were not so fruitful.

Cooperation between the British ground and air forces was developed to a highly efficient standard during the desert battles, the fighter playing an increasingly important part through being vectored to attack targets requested by the Army, often at short notice. Having blunted Rommel's ambitions in the first Battle of El Alamein, the British 8th Army opened a massive attack at this location on the night of 23/24 October 1942, driving their old adversary back to Tripolitania for the last time. At the start of this battle the *Luftwaffe* had some 325 aircraft available and the Italians 250, as against approximately a thousand with the British Commonwealth and newly arrived

**Left, upper:** Hurricanes of No 274 Squadron in an attack formation. The wing-up action, slowly rocking from side to side, of the trailing aircraft in the string was to guard against surprise attack from beneath. It was a general precept of fighter interception that if an enemy was seen in time it was possible to take successful evasive action. The problem was the restricted outlook from a fighter cockpit. The most cautious time was flying with the sun behind, for even with dark glasses it was often impossible to see assailants approach until it was too late to evade. (IWM CM132)

**Left, lower:** No 33 Squadron was the second unit in the Middle East to convert fully from Gladiators to Hurricanes at Fuka in September and October 1940. P3726, under maintenance in the foreground, was written off in a crash with No 71 OTU the following year. Flying this aircraft on 11 December 1940, Flight Lieutenant Charles Dyson surprised an Italian formation when he emerged from cloud. He claimed six CR.42 biplane fighters, one of which brought down an SM.79 bomber as it fell. (IWM CM140)

**Below:** In August 1940 No 3 Squadron RAAF arrived in the Middle East; the unit was in action by November. Fighter aircraft were scarce and initially the squadron had a mixed complement of Gloster Gauntlets and Gladiators, eventually standardising on the latter type. Four Gladiators, led by Flying Officer Alan Rawlinson, were returning from a tactical reconnaissance on 19 November when they encountered eighteen Fiat CR.42s in the Rabia area and a 20-minute dogfight, reminiscent of those fought in the First World War, ensued. Rawlinson (left) shot down one of the Fiats, Flight Lieutenant B. R. Pelly (centre) had two probables and Flying Officer Alan Boyd (right) destroyed two, using N5752/NW:G shown. The code letters were those of No 33 Squadron, with which this Gladiator II previously served. The fourth Gladiator pilot was lost in this action. The squadron was not so fortunate the following month when, on the 13th, five of its Gladiators were shot down in another fight with CR.42s. Alan Boyd claimed his fourth and fifth victories on this occasion but was in one of the Gladiators shot down. He managed to crash-land in the desert and returned to his unit having sustained only minor injuries. (IWM CM245)

USAAF units. The American fighter contribution was a group of P-40F Warhawks. A USAAF fighter group normally consisted of three squadrons and approximated to an RAF wing. The P-40F was similar to the RAF Kittyhawk, an improved Tomahawk, but powered by the Packard V-1650 engine, a licence-built version of the Rolls-Royce Merlin 60 engine with two-stage supercharger. The P-40F had a far superior performance at higher altitudes than the earlier model. At this time the RAF Desert Air Force had two squadrons of Tomahawks, six with Kittyhawks, four with Hurricanes and one with Spitfire Vs, in total some 350 fighters. Among 700 combat aircraft the *Luftwaffe* had 120 Me 109Fs which could only be matched by the twenty Spitfire Vs, though not above 20,000ft. At least for the first time the Desert Air Force squadrons were receiving aircraft which were not markedly inferior to the opposition's.

In the twelve days of fighting, until the *Afrika Korps* was in full retreat, the Desert Air Force lost 97 aircraft of all types and the Germans and Italians 84. There was no question as to who held the sky, and while strength of numbers told, better tactics played a significant part. Such was the confidence of Air Vice-Marshal Arthur Coningham, the Desert Air Force commander, that he sent two Hurricane squadrons to a secret desert airstrip far ahead of the front line to harass Rommel's retreating columns for two days.

**Above:** The Fiat CR.42's performance was on a par with the Gladiator's but its two 12.7mm machine guns proved a more effective armament than the Gladiator's four rifle-calibre weapons. However, the doughty Italian biplane was no match for the Hurricane, and *Regia Aeronautica* units with the type suffered severely during the air fighting of 1941. This CR.42 down near Bardia was the victim of a Hurricane pilot. (IWM CM319)

**Left:** There was often no water to spare for men's toilet in the frequent moves of base that the campaigns in the Western Desert demanded, and in consequence beards flourished. Flying Officer Ernest M. Mason sports 'Balbo' facial growth as he rests exhausted at Gazala after shooting down three CR.42s west of Martuba on 26 January 1941. The highest-scoring Hurricane pilot in No 274 Squadron during the 8th Army's first offensive into Libya, Ernie Mason shot down fourteen enemy aircraft in seven weeks. (The pre-war flying suit he is wearing carries the emblem of No 80 Squadron, with

which he previously served.) Mason later flew Hurricanes in Malta, where he was shot down into the sea. Promoted, in January 1942 he was posted to command No 94 Squadron flying Kittyhawks but lost his life on 15 February when he and three other pilots of his squadron were shot down by an Me 109F while on a strafing raid. (IWM CM422)

**Above:** Another notable No 274 Squadron pilot was Flight Lieutenant Dudley Honor, who had seen combat in France and England during 1940 before being posted to the Middle East. With a 44 Imp gallon tank under each wing, the squadron's aircraft flew a number of long-range sorties from Gerawla in support of British forces on Crete in May 1941. On the 25th Honor destroyed two transports over Maleme and was then attacked by *Luftwaffe* fighters and shot down into the sea. His Hurricane, W9266, submerged instantly, but, escaping from the cockpit, Honor swam towards Crete, which took nearly four hours to reach. Unobserved by enemy forces, he rested before finding his way to a British-held part of the island. It took six days before he managed to pass safely through enemy lines, where he was rescued by a Sunderland. The lightning flash on the fuselage of the Hurricane was the unofficial squadron insignia when code letters were discontinued for a period in 1941. Note how sand abrasion has taken the paint from the propeller blades. (IWM CH941)

**Left:** One of the few known service photographs of Squadron Leader M. T. St J. Pattle, who was the RAF's highest scoring fighter ace of the Second World War. He is on the left; the other man is believed to be No 33 Squadron's Intelligence Officer. The exact total of Pattle's victories has never been established owing to the dearth of records for forces operating in Greece during 1941. 'Pat' Pattle flew Gladiators with No 80 Squadron there and previously in North Africa, with some 15 known victories. From February 1941 he was flying Hurricanes, being promoted to command No 33 Squadron the following month. During the heavy fighting of the next few weeks he claimed at least another 35 enemy aircraft, finally to be shot down himself and killed by Me 110s in an air fight over Eleusis Bay near Athens on 20 April 1941. Nevertheless, although his score has been put at tentative 45 by experts who have investigated the matter, Pattle's record is certainly unsurpassed by any other RAF pilot. (IWM ME1260)

**Left:** Many records were lost during the hurried exodus from Crete, the photographer's notes identifying these pilots resting beside No 274 Squadron Hurricane V7589/YK:Q being an example. (IWM ME1088)

**Above:** With the arrival in Libya of *JG 27* and its Me 109Fs, the *Luftwaffe* had a fighter far superior to the Hurricanes and Tomahawks of the RAF. Claimed to be the first example of the type brought down, this aircraft is being prepared for transportation to the Canal Zone for examination. (IWM CM1972)

**Below:** The Hurricane was the mainstay of Malta's air defence during 1941 and losses were high. Z5265/T, seen at Hal Far, served with No 185 Squadron until shot down north of Gozo on 30 September 1941. (IWM CM1356)

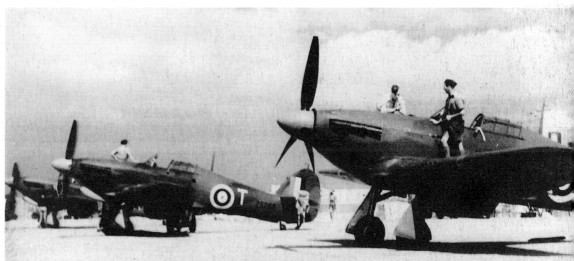

**Above:** Tomahawk GA:J of No 112 Squadron in the hands of fitters and riggers. Work frequently had to be performed without the benefit of shade and often with primitive aids. No 112's Tomahawks operated with a decorative 'shark' nose as a unit marking, as can be seen on the removed radiator intake cowling. The Tomahawk may have had an inferior performance to that of the Me 109F, but, used with skill, it proved that its principal antagonist could be bested. The two machine guns mounted over the engine and synchronised to fire through the propeller could often be used to advantage as they did not have the ranging problems inherent in wing-mounted weapons. (IWM CM2039)

**Left:** Spares were frequently unavailable at desert landing grounds in Tripolitania and the cannibalisation of damaged aircraft considered beyond economical repair was frequently undertaken to meet the shortage. Tomahawk AN420/ GL:P of No 5 Squadron SAAF suffered this fate but was eventually rebuilt and sent to No 73 OTU. (IWM CM4409)

**Right:** On 3 July 1942, in the El Alamein area, No 1 Squadron of the South African Air Force intercepted a formation of fifteen Ju 87s escorted by Me 109Fs. In the ensuing fight the squadron's Hurricanes claimed thirteen *Stukas* and an Me 109 shot down without loss, the Messerschmitts, apparently being distracted by other Allied aircraft, arriving too late effectively to intervene. Here the CO, 38-year-old Major Gerald le Mesurier, who destroyed the first *Stuka*, poses beside his Hurricane II, BG971/AX:V, at LG 92. The following day, while intercepting another Ju 87 raid, le Mesurier was shot down and badly wounded near El Imayid in this aircraft by an Me 109F of *I/JG 27*. Eventually declared unfit for further combat operations, he came to Britain, where he was killed in an air accident in July 1943. (IWM CM3027)

**Left:** Twenty-year-old Flight Sergeant George Beurling claimed 26 enemy aircraft shot down during a four-month period flying Spitfires of No 249 Squadron in defence of Malta. A somewhat unruly character, he lived for flying and did not take kindly to the necessary authority of command, earning the nickname 'Screwball'. Reluctantly commissioned, he was shot down and wounded on 14 October 1942, baling out to be rescued from the sea. While he was being transferred to Britain for convalescence the transport in which he was flying came down in the sea off Gibraltar but he managed to swim ashore. After he had recovered he flew operationally with Nos 403 and 412 Squadrons in England, claiming two more victories for a total of 31 destroyed and one shared. Insubordination was the apparent reason for his being returned to his native Canada in the spring of 1944 and later being discharged from the RCAF. A restless soul, in 1948 Beurling sought to fly for Israel but was killed en route when the aircraft which he was ferrying exploded soon after take-off from Rome. When this photograph was taken in Malta, a journalist described Beurling as being 'tall with an expressionless face and enormous eyes which have a slightly faraway look in them. His hair is long and bleached by the sun and is always falling in his eyes, except when topped by a flying helmet . . . Screwball neither drinks nor smokes. He is not the least bit talkative and is incommunicative about himself to the last degree.' (IWM CM3658)

**Left:** Many aircraft that had been crash-landed in the desert could be repaired. Repair and Salvage Unit teams with articulated lorries set out to collect these and return them to one of the major maintenance depots in the Canal Zone. On this occasion, when a teabreak was called, Hurricanes from Nos 73, 80, 94 and 229 Squadrons fill the convoy's lorries. The No 229 Squadron aircraft, Z4967/HB:D, has signs of cannon-shell damage in its rudder. (IWM CM2232)

**Below:** A Hurricane of No 73 Squadron lifted by crane on to a tender from where it crash-landed in the desert in January 1942. For a period during 1941 and 1942 squadron code letters were discontinued by most Middle East units with the object of concealing the disposition of RAF strength. No 73 was one of a few squadrons that then used unofficial markings, in its case the blue and yellow flash that had marked its pre-war aircraft. Hurricane BD930 was repaired and served with Nos 335 and 127 Squadrons the following year. (IWM CM2240)

**Right:** Lady Rachel MacRobert lost three sons, one before the war in a flying accident and two with the RAF in 1941. This resilient woman promptly funded the purchase of a Stirling heavy bomber and four Hurricane fighters. Three of the latter were named after her sons and the fourth, with the slogan 'Salute to Russia', was called *The Lady.* In September 1942 all initially flew with No 94 Squadron, with which Sir Roderick MacRobert was serving when killed. This aircraft, BP635, was usually flown by Flight Lieutenant John Barber, who is seen here with the aircraft at El Gamil. (IWM CM3419)

**Below:** Victor and vanquished: a Hurricane parked near the tail of an Fw 200 *Kurier* transport destroyed at Castel Benito. There was an ample supply of Hurricanes in North Africa by 1943, and this aircraft was used as a run-around by No 2 Photographic Reconnaissance Unit. (IWM CM4538)

**Right:** The first USAAF fighter unit to become operational with the Middle East US Ninth Air Force was the 57th Fighter Group. Its three squadrons, equipped with P-40F Warhawks, took part in the Second Battle of El Alamein in October 1942 and followed the British Army as it advanced into Tripolitania. Two other P-40 groups, the 79th and the 324th, also joined the Ninth Air Force but did not go into action until the British advance reached Tunisia. These are 86th Fighter Squadron/79th Fighter Group P-40Fs under maintenance and repair at Causeway Landing Ground near the western border of Libya. The nearest Warhawk is undergoing an engine change. (IWM CM4928)

# 9
# 'TORCH' AND 'HUSKY'

On 8 November 1942 the combined British and American invasion of North-West Africa, known by the code-name 'Torch', was launched with parachute troops and seaborne landings. Airfield bases were soon acquired in French Morocco and Algeria and a sizeable force of aircraft, including some 220 fighters, was brought in to support the ground forces. The RAF contingent included 90 Spitfire Vs in six squadrons transferred from Fighter Command, and there were 130 of the same mark in six American-manned squadrons previously assigned to the US Eighth Air Force in Britain. All had been shipped by sea to Gibraltar, reassembled and flown to Algerian airfields soon after the invasion was launched. The RAF also commited two squadrons of Hurricane IICs. Longer-ranged aircraft were flown down from England to stage through Gibraltar, including five squadrons of Lockheed P-38F Lightnings and two of Beaufighter IVFs for night defence. Other units were to follow, the RAF's Eastern Air Command soon having over 500 aircraft and the US Twelfth Air Force 1,300.

Endeavours to conceal preparations for this enterprise were unsuccessful, and although the Germans did not know where the build-up at Gibraltar was heading until the actual landings occurred, they immediately took measures to increase their forces in North Africa. Within a few days several thousand troops had been airlifted into Tunisia and *Luftwaffe* fighter and ground support units deployed in that country. From just over 700 combat aircraft in the general Mediterranean area in October 1942, the *Luftwaffe*'s strength was nearly doubled within three months. Owing to difficulties in establishing the extended line of supply and unusually wet weather, the Allied advance made slow progress and was halted by the *Wehrmacht* near the Tunisian/Algerian border.

The Allied fighter squadrons, moved to forward airfields, discovered that they would have to do battle with experienced Me 109G *Gruppen*. In fact, the spread of Allied forces found the *Luftwaffe* well able to sustain a masterly defence. Once again the Me 109 *Experten* could use their well-tried tactics of

**Left:** A 48th Fighter Squadron P-38F flown by Captain Ralph Watson after landing at Gibraltar on 10 November 1942 having flown from England. A 150 US gallon auxiliary tank on each wing pylon gave ample fuel for the thousand-mile flight. The 48th was a unit of the 14th Fighter Group, which began operations from North African bases the next day. (USAAF)

**Right:** The wreckage of a French naval fighter being removed by US personnel at Port Lyautey, on or about 12 November 1942. French opposition to the landings at Casablanca resulted in the shelling and bombing of this airfield, which consequently required much crater-filling before it could be used safely. In the background is P-40F 41-14270, *Belchin' Bessie,* of the 33rd Fighter Group. The 33rd was transported directly from America on the carrier USS *Chenango*, flying its 76 ferried Warhawks off to land at this base. A Stars and Stripes flag is painted under the left wing as it was thought this would be more familiar to the French than the *cocarde* marking. (USAAF)

dive, attack, dive and recover, bringing heavy losses to some of the neophyte Allied units, particularly those with the P-38 Lightning. The P-38 was at the time of its first flight in 1939 an advanced design holding great promise. A series of development problems delayed production, and updating to meet combat requirements stole some of its promise through increased weight. The unusual configuration of a central pod for pilot and armament, placed between two engines heading fuselage booms, was novel and allowed excellent streamlining. Unfortunately, the tailplane linking the booms caused buffeting in high-speed dives, a problem that was never satisfactorily overcome. However, for a relatively large aircraft, the P-38 could turn with a Spitfire V at slow speeds, was as fast and was a much better gun platform with its nose-mounted armament of a 20mm cannon and four .50-calibre machine guns. Pilots liked it, particularly as the propellers were contra-rotating, making directional stability excellent. Alas, fighter-versus-fighter combat was more often than not at high speed and did not involve a turning contest.

One P-38 group, which only had two squadrons, was sent to Youks-les-Bains near the central Tunisian border, where a squadron from the other P-38 group, retained further back from the front for escorting bombers, joined it in late November. These squadrons were chiefly engaged in affording air cover for the ground forces and suffered cruelly: by late December a third of the original force had been destroyed or written off due to accident. Two other P-38 groups had arrived in Britain, and in December one of these was sent on to North Africa, where, initially, its aircraft and pilots were used to make good the losses in the other two groups. But P-38 attrition continued at

a high rate, and on 28 January 1943 the two squadrons of the first group to go into action were so depleted that they were withdrawn. Of their original 54 pilots who had arrived in North Africa in November, 32 had been killed or were missing, 23 of them in air combat, and at this time only 130 P-38s remained of some 210 that had been sent to Africa. The USAAF had hoped to retain the remaining Lightning group in England for bomber escort but the situation for both P-38s and their pilots was so critical that all those in England were sent to North Africa in February.

For both fighter and fighter-bomber work a group of P-40F Warhawks, brought from the United States on a carrier, was so heavily involved in the actions on the American sector that of its 75 aircraft only 13 were left serviceable by the end of January, the rest having been shot down or written off. This group was also withdrawn to re-form. Sturdy and reliable, the P-40s fell mostly to ground fire rather than enemy fighters. Two other US fighter groups were brought from England in December and January but through poor navigation and unexpected high winds several aircraft put down in Portugal and were interned. Both groups were equipped with Bell Airacobras, P-39D and P-400 versions, which on British advice were to be employed in ground attack or on duties where single-engine enemy fighters were unlikely to be encountered, the Airacobra's performance being much inferior to that of the Me 109G in all respects.

The stalemate in North Africa, in some part due to the terrain and poor winter weather, brought a reassessment of the air campaign with the objective of obtaining complete air superiority. A High Command appraisal identified the need for a

**Above:** A test-run for Spitfire VC EP788 at Gibraltar in November 1942, following assembly for the North African air forces. Aircraft arriving by sea freight in packing cases each took, on average, a day to make ready. EP788 eventually was sent to the USSR. (IWM CM6700)
**Left:** A bogged-down 350th Fighter Group Bell P-39D Airacobra, 42-4581, languishes in Algerian mud at Oujda. Considered too vulnerable in fighter duties, the units with this type were confined chiefly to coastal patrol and armed reconnaissance. (USAAF)

more integrated Allied command, the British and American contingents having to some extent served their own individual requirements during the early stages of the campaign. In February 1943 the US Twelfth Air Force, RAF Desert Air Force and Eastern Air Command came under an overall command called the North-West African Air Forces, headed by Major-General Carl Spaatz. New units were brought in, and by mid-March the Allies had some 1,500 aircraft on hand, including six more RAF Spitfire squadrons from Britain and four P-40 squadrons for the Twelfth Air Force. The *Luftwaffe* had also increased its numbers, having six *Gruppen* of Me 109Gs which, with two dedicated *Jabo Staffeln*, totalled around 200 aircraft. A more worrying discovery for the Allies was the presence of Fw 190s, but it transpired that these were mostly *Jabos* with a ground attack mission. Nevertheless, this brought hastily formed special flights with Spitfire IXs to two Spitfire squadrons.

With the renewed ground battles, better direction, better tactics, better equipment and not least greater numbers brought the Allied fighters air superiority. Realising that defeat was only a matter of time, the *Wehrmacht* began withdrawing from its diminishing hold on Tunisia. In April 1943 Allied fighters were often able to intercept the Ju 52/3m, Me 323 and other lumbering transport aircraft, being credited with shooting down 141 during the month. The last *Luftwaffe* units to withdraw were the Me 109s and some Italian MC.205s. Between the opening of 'Torch' and the final May 1943 withdrawals, approximately 2,500 Axis aircraft had been lost. During the same period the Allies lost a similar number of aircraft to all causes.

Having ejected the German and Italian forces from Africa, the Western Allies went on to invade Sicily in July 1943, in Operation 'Husky'. The island fortress of Malta, so long a thorn in the Axis side, now proved invaluable as the only base from which Spitfire IXs could provide cover over the eastern landing places, being only 55 miles away. The US landing

**Right:** The *Luftwaffe* hits back. A P-38F of the 1st Fighter Group was destroyed in a night raid on Biskra, Algeria, during December 1942. Here personnel examine the burnt-out wreckage the morning after the attack. (USAAF)

beaches were covered from the Maltese island of Gozo and ex-Italian Pantelleria. Three squadrons of US Spitfire Vs, which had met with much success during the North African fighting, operated from Gozo and three squadrons of Warhawks flew from Pantelleria. *Luftwaffe* fighter opposition was minimal in comparison with North African activities, partly because many of the *Jagdgruppen* were withdrawn to combat the increasing daylight bombing activities of the Americans in western Europe.

With an overwhelming force of a thousand fighters and fighter-bombers, the Allies completed the conquest of Sicily by early August, the German and Italian forces withdrawing across the Straits of Messina (only three miles separates Sicily from Italy at this point). By concentrating anti-aircraft weapons at the ports, and thanks to a spirited cover by some 80 Me 109s, 39,500 Axis troops were able to escape. The Allies lost little time in following, the first landings in Italy by the British 8th Army being made on 3 September with minimal opposition. Italy surrendered unconditionally five days later and the following day a major amphibious operation was carried out to establish the US Fifth Army at Salerno further up the coast. This outflanking move met with strong opposition, not least in the air, where cover was difficult to provide: the Spitfire IXs had only 20–25 minutes' patrol time, and that carrying long-range drop tanks.

P-38s, with their larger drop tanks, could stay for a hour. Even so, the Me 109Gs could only make limited interceptions in an effort to divert attention from the *Jabos*. A serious situation was eventually relieved by the Allied advance from Messina and the *Wehrmacht* withdrew to a defensive line in the moun-

**Above:** 'It was a gamble whether I bale out' was Squadron Leader Lance Wade's comment on the damage inflicted by an Me 109 on Spitfire IX EN186 after he had shot down another Me 109 while providing top cover for Kittyhawks attacking shipping off Cape Bon on 30 April 1943. Texas-born 'Wildcat' Wade volunteered for the RAF in 1940 and was sent to the Middle East, where he distinguished himself by shooting down twelve and damaging several more enemy aircraft. A second tour took him back to North Africa, where, in command of No 145 Squadron, he raised his total of air victories to 22 and two shared. Tragically he was killed on 12 January 1944 in an air accident involving the Auster he was flying. No other US national who served only with the RAF had a larger number of air victories than the dynamic Lance C. Wade. (IWM CE64)

tains south of Rome. The remaining *Jagdgruppen* in Italy could muster no more than 150 fighters by November. The forces opposing them now included a growing number of Spitfire IXs, for which the RAF and Dominion squadrons engaged in the Sicilian and Italian campaigns had priority during the summer of 1943. The US Spitfire fighter squadrons would also receive this superior mark. But the major fighter activity in Europe was now again concentrated in the north-west.

**Left:** Flight Sergeant Roy Hussey and No 72 Squadron's Intelligence Officer, Pilot Officer Simm, examine part of the fuselage of an Me 109G. The enemy fighter was shot down by Hussey on 20 December 1942 during a *Luftwaffe* raid on the landing ground at Souka el Arba. Hussey was eventually credited with destroying ten enemy aircraft, only to lose his life in an accident on 20 February 1945 flying a Mustang of No 19 Squadron. ( IWM CNA127)

**Above:** No 154 Squadron, associated with British Motor Industries, was one of the Spitfire squadrons sent from Britain to North Africa following the 'Torch' landings. Here a Mk VC, ER676/HT:E, undergoes maintenance and re-arming at Souk el Khemis in April 1943. On the 25th of that month, with Sergeant. J Sillitoe, it failed to return from escorting B-25s over the Gulf of Tunis. (IWM CNA 602)

**Right:** The appearance of the Fw 190 over Tunisia, and the knowledge that its performance was far superior to that of the Spitfire V equipping RAF and USAAF squadrons, brought a special Spitfire IX flight, hurried down from Britain. It was formed by Polish ace Stanislaw Skalski and attached to No 145 Squadron. Skalski added three enemy aircraft to his tally during this period. He is seen here taxying out in EN315/ZX:6, the Spitfire usually flown by Flight Lieutenant Horbaczewski, another member of the flight. (IWM CNA4542)

**Left:** Squadron Leader John J. Lynch was responsible for what at the time was hailed as the 1,000th air victory achieved by Allied pilots flying from Malta. This occurred on 28 April 1943 when Lynch shot down a Ju 52/3m transport off Cap Cafafu. An American volunteer for the RAF, he began his operational career with the Eagle Squadrons on cross-Channel sorties. Posted to Malta at the end of 1942, he had several victories with No 249 Squadron, eventually becoming its CO. When his tour was completed, at which time he had ten victories, plus seven shared, Lynch was transferred to the USAAF, although he saw no more combat in the Second World War. Like several distinguished veterans of that conflict, he lost his life in a post-war flying accident. (IWM CM5096)

**Right:** The RAF fighter pilot personified: Flight Lieutenant Charles 'Sammy' Samoulle, DFC and Bar, shortly after his return from North Africa where, serving with No 92 Squadron, he had 18 claims against enemy aircraft, of which seven were confirmed destroyed. He went on to fly the powerful Spitfire XIV, claiming three more aircraft destroyed and two damaged in the air with No 130 Squadron. (IWM CH11400)

# 10
# THE QUEST FOR RANGE

German air activity over Britain following Hitler's invasion of the USSR was confined chiefly to night bombing sorties on a limited scale and *Jabo* attacks in the coastal areas of south-east England. The night fighter version of the de Havilland Mosquito began to replace the Beaufighter in 1942 as the principal type for combating the night bomber, the Beaufighter being transferred to the Mediterranean and Far East where its air-cooled engines were better suited to operating from 'dirt' airfields. The Mosquito was as fast as the Hurricane and packed a four-cannon, four-machine-gun armament in the nose. Its principle advantage over the Beaufighter for night fighting was that pilot and radar observer sat side by side, if somewhat cramped, providing much better cooperation in finding a target aircraft. AI radar development had advanced to the Mk VIII set which could pick up a raider from 2,000yds and retain an image to firing distance. The night sky over Britain became even more dangerous for the *Luftwaffe*.

*Jabo* attacks were now carried out with Fw 190s, usually at very low altitudes to avoid radar detection. The best chance of intercepting these fighter-bomber raids was the costly business of standing patrols, for which Typhoons were usually detailed. Overall, the Typhoon was a disappointment to Fighter Command. As already noted, its introduction to squadron service was delayed by development problems, not least with the powerful Napier Sabre engine, rated at 2,400hp. The promise of a top speed of 400mph was met, but only at low altitude, and the aircraft's general performance was disappointing, being inferior in most requirements to that of the latest mark of Spitfire. More disappointing were the number of problems encountered in the squadrons with early production aircraft. Carbon monoxide fumes entered the cockpit, tails broke off in high-speed manoeuvres and engines seized, causing many fatalities. Indeed, it was estimated that during the first eighteen months of service more Typhoon pilots were killed in accidents than as a result of enemy action. Modifications to engine exhausts and improved cockpit sealing failed to eradicate completely the problem of fumes, resulting in the Typhoon pilot having to use of oxygen from engine start-up to shut-down as SOP. A pro-

**Right:** Thunderbolt firepower. There was nothing new about eight-gun fighters by December 1942, but the P-47Cs that began arriving in Britain that month had 0.50in Brownings with much greater destructive power than the rifle-calibre weapons used in British fighters early in the war. The 'point-fifty' had its origins as an infantry weapon during the First World War. Surprisingly, the USAAF preferred this weapon to cannon for its single-engine fighters. (S. Clay Collection)

gramme of strengthening the rear fuselage just forward of the tailplane was introduced, but tailplane failures still occurred, if not so frequently. Sleeve-valve fracture was eventually established as the main cause of the engine malfunctions, and this trouble was not satisfactorily dealt with until the summer 1943, by which time squadron Typhoons were limited to a set number of engine hours per month. The drag of the Typhoon's relatively thick aerofoil may have been a poor choice for a high-performance fighter, but the sturdy wing was soon recognised as an excellent platform for stores. Wing racks and the Sabre's power at low altitude permitted two 500lb bombs to be carried with ease, and the Typhoon had the makings of an excellent fighter-bomber. The first two squadrons with this mission were formed in the autumn of 1942, and during the following year most Typhoon squadrons went over to this role. Hurricane and Whirlwind squadrons with this mission were soon converted to the 'Tiffy'.

Fighter-bombing and other forms of ground attack were a regular feature of Fighter Command's cross-Channel operations during 1942 and 1943, for which the major limiting factor was radius of action rather than enemy opposition. Despite being depleted by a sizeable force transferred to Mediterranean theatre commands from autumn 1942, Fighter Command still had 63 day fighter squadrons with over a thousand aircraft by the following spring. There were also sixteen fighter-reconnaissance squadrons in the soon to be disbanded Army Co-operation Command, fourteen equipped with the Mustang I, which bolstered the numbers of day fighters by another 300. Only the Mustangs had a significant radius of action on inter-

nal fuel, some 400 miles, whereas the Spitfires, Typhoons, Whirlwinds and Hurricanes were limited to between 125 and 200 miles from their bases. However, as the RAF had no requirement for a long-range fighter—its Chief having accepted that such would be unable to compete with a short-range interceptor—the Mustangs were used for army support where, in patrolling over front lines, endurance was a valuable asset. True, the Allison-engine Mustang had shown an inferior performance to the Me 109F and Fw 190A in comparison tests, particularly at high altitudes, but it was the only fighter type in squadron service that could match the enemy fighter's dive. In their fighter-reconnaissance role Mustang Is were chiefly confined to long-range Rhubarbs for the best part of two years.

By 1943 the fact that such a large force of day fighters reposed in Great Britain with such a limited access to combat began to trouble the British War Cabinet and the RAF leadership. Measures were taken to make more use of auxiliary fuel tanks that could be jettisoned when emptied. New Spitfires were given small wing tanks in the leading edges to expand endurance. The most interesting development, originally suggested by a Rolls-Royce test pilot, was the replacement of the Allison engine in the Mustang by a 60-series Merlin, with the prospect of both good range and high performance. Moreover, the matter of range was given a new emphasis by the coming of the US Eighth Air Force and its daylight bombing activities.

When the B-17 Fortresses began their high-level bombing missions in summer 1942 support was given by RAF Fighter Command, although the high-altitude self-defending formations were expected to look after themselves in hostile airspace. Indeed, the first few raids indicated that the B-17s could do just that, experiencing little interference from the *Luftwaffe*. This immunity was short-lived, for while the *Jagdgruppen* did find these high-flying, tight formations with massed defensive fire difficult to tackle, it was not long before the American bombers were recognised as a formidable threat and *Luftwaffe* day fighter forces in the west were substantially increased. RAF Fighter Command then had a new task for its Spitfires, flying escort and diversionary sweeps to aid the Fortresses and Liberators, although, still only having around a hundred Spitfire IXs for much of the winter because of the Mediterranean priority, there was a limit to the high-altitude protection available. Climbing to 30,000ft and flying at high speed reduced endurance appreciably.

Until January 1943 the Eighth Air Force's targets were in occupied territory, where Fighter Command support could cover the bombers for part of the way. Over Germany and on deeper penetrations into France, where there were no Spitfires to worry about, the *Jagdflieger* began to take a toll of the American bombers. The Eighth Air Force's commander, Brigadier-General Ira Eaker, although having a fighter background, believed that given strength of numbers his bombers would not suffer prohibitive losses on their missions. Nevertheless, he wished to give the bombers as much fighter support as possible, requesting P-38 Lightnings which had an escort potential of 400 miles from base using drop tanks. Not only was P-38 production quite unable to keep up with demand, the critical situation in the Mediterranean Theatre of Operations (MTO) gave that war zone priority during the winter of 1942 and the following spring. The only American type available with some range advantage over the Spitfire was the Republic P-47C Thunderbolt. Moreover, the P-47 had been literally designed around a turbo-supercharger installation to give best performance at sub-stratosphere altitudes. In December 1942 the first P-47Cs arrived in England, initially to convert the sole US-manned Spitfire V group, re-equip the group that had its P-38s and pilots sent to North Africa as replacements and fill out the first fighter group to fly the type in the United States, which arrived in Britain at this time. The three groups—nine squadrons—did not become fully operational until April 1943, partly because of difficulties with engine ignition disrupting radio communication.

**Opposite:** A new shape in British skies: Republic P-47C Thunderbolts of the 62nd Fighter Squadron over Kingscliffe in March 1943. Designed as a high-altitude interceptor, the P-47 was capable of 430mph at 30,000ft although its appetite at this speed was in the region of 300 US gallons an hour. This photograph was taken at the time special high-visibility markings were introduced to distinguish the P-47 from the Fw 190, although there was little resemblance to the *Luftwaffe* fighter other than its having a blunt, radial-engine nose. The P-47 with the white nose and tail bands, 41-6189, was lost in August 1943. (S. Clay Collection)

**Right:** The 4th Fighter Group, the ex-RAF Eagle Squadrons, began conversion to the P-47 at Debden in January 1943. Its pilots were generally not enthusiastic about the comparative giant and were loath to give up their Spitfires. A particular complaint was the Thunderbolt's relatively slow climb. Here Lieutenant James Goodson, who had two air victories in Spitfires, goes out to gain experience in flying the Thunderbolt. He went on to claim five enemy aircraft flying the type and another nine at the controls of a Mustang. By June 1944 Goodson was also the leading Eighth Air Force ground strafer with fifteen *Luftwaffe* aircraft destroyed on their bases. Like many other fighter pilots, he was eventually brought down by flak while strafing and taken prisoner. (USAAF)

Comparison tests with the RAF's captured Fw 190A and Me 109F indicated that the P-47C was no match below 15,000ft. However, the higher the altitude the more the Thunderbolt's performance improved, and at 30,000ft it could outpace both enemy types thanks to the powerful turbo-supercharged engine. On the debit side, its rate of climb was, by comparison, abysmal. The Fw 190A took approximately eleven minutes to reach 25,000ft, the Me 109G seven minutes and the Spitfire IX six minutes against fifteen minutes for the P-47C. The main reason for a Thunderbolt taking twice as long as an Me 109G or Spitfire IX was its size and weight, about double that of the British and German fighters in both respects. The American fighter's armament consisted of eight wing-mounted 0.50in machine guns, which had three times the effective range of rifle-calibre weapons and in consequence much more destructive power at closer ranges. The rate of fire was slightly lower, but the battery of eight guns was formidable. There were no explosive rounds, armour-piercing incendiary having proved the more destructive.

The Thunderbolt squadrons did not have a very auspicious entry into combat. The Americans initially adopted RAF formation and escort tactics, the *Jagdgruppen* responding with the usual dive and run attacks on occasions when an advantage was observed. Although the *Luftwaffe* increased fighter defence in the west to a total of more than 600 single-engine and 400 twin-engine aircraft during the spring and summer of 1943, Allied fighter activity was avoided rather than challenged in order to concentrate attacks on the Eighth Air Force heavy bombers. The American Fortresses were pushing further into the *Reich* to conduct precision attacks on selected targets, mostly factories and depots having some connection with aircraft production. The bombing, while often inaccurate, caused sufficient destruction at some locations to make this development in the air war of major concern to the Germans. This was partly countered by increasing the armament of the Me 109G, which was the principal interceptor of these high-altitude raids. The 20mm cannon placed between the engine cylinder banks and firing through the propeller shaft was replaced with a remarkable 30mm weapon, the MK 108. A single round from this gun had four times the explosive power of a 20mm round, and was delivered at approximately the same rate of fire, 600 rounds per minute. Additionally some Me 109Gs had a 30mm or 20mm cannon in a fairing under each wing, while the rifle-calibre 7.9mm machine guns above the engine were replaced by 13mm weapons, equivalent to the American .50 guns. Unlike both the British and Americans, the Germans developed guns exclusively as aircraft weapons. The disadvantage of this increased armament was the increase in weight, adversely affecting the Me 109G's handling and robbing the model of the ascendancy it once possessed in comparison with some Allied fighters.

Despite increasingly heavy bomber losses, Eighth Air Force commanders believed that the B-17 and B-24 gunners were

**Right:** The two Whirlwind squadrons were relegated to fighter-bombing with low-level trips to and from the target. No 137 Squadron was engaged in this work while based at Manston from September 1942 until the supply of Whirlwinds dwindled and the unit had to convert to Hurricane IVs in the following June. Usually flown by Flight Lieutenant L. H. Bartlett, Whirlwind P6993/SF:A is shown orbiting Manston. It met its end on 22 June 1943 after suffering engine failure and crash-landing near Sandwich. (MOI)

**Below:** Many RAF squadrons had a mix of nationalities and No 263 Squadron was one of these. This, the first and last squadron with Westland Whirlwinds, had Indian, West Indian, Australian and Canadian as well as British pilots assigned during spring 1943. Seen here with Flight Lieutenant Geoffrey B. Warnes (second left), who became CO in December that year, are the Adjutant, Flight Lieutenant E. C. Owens, on Warnes' right; Flight Lieutenant H.

K. Blackshaw on Warnes' left; then Sergeant S. D. Thyagarajan from India; Flying Officer C. P. King from the West Indies; Flight Sergeant F. L. Hicks from Australia; and Flying Officer J. P. Cayne from Canada. 'Glass Eye' Warnes, so called because of his use of contact lenses to overcome short-sightedness, was a much venerated member of the squadron. No 263 converted to Typhoons and on 22 February 1944, when returning from a sweep, Warnes was forced to ditch, believed due to engine failure. He was seen to get out of the aircraft but to be in difficulties. Thereupon another member of the flight, Pilot Officer R. B. Tuff, in an unprecedented act of bravery, baled out with the intention of helping his CO. Neither man was seen again. No 263 Squadron was designated 'The Fellowship of the Bellows' squadron, since a number of its aircraft were funded from this association in South America. With the object of 'raising the wind' for the RAF, each fellow paid one centimo for every enemy aircraft destroyed claimed by the RAF, and the funds so raised were used to pay for another fighter. Whirlwind P7094/HE:T, usually flown by Blackshaw, carries an acknowledgement below the cockpit. (IWM CH8986)

**Right:** Given a fighter-reconnaissance role, the Mustang I rendered excellent service to the end of hostilities. This No 4 Squadron aircraft, AP247/A, endured in squadron service from October 1942 through to VE-Day, having been passed to No 309 and then No 26 Squadron, the last to fly this model. When photographed this particular Mustang was being demonstrated over Bottisham in April 1943 by, it is believed, Wing Commander G. E. Macdonald, whose personal mount it was. The Mustang's substantial armament of two nose-mounted 0.50-calibre machine guns, another in each wing, plus two .303-calibre in each wing, shows in this picture. (S. Clay Collection)

extracting a crippling toll of *Luftwaffe* fighters. Unfortunately, nowhere during Second World War air fighting were the claims of aircraft destroyed, probably destroyed and damaged more exaggerated than with these Eighth Air Force bomber missions. The reason was simply that in the heat of battle perhaps a score of air gunners would fire at the same intercepting fighter and each would be convinced that it was his fire that did the damage. It was clear that there was considerable over-claiming, but the exact extent was not known until after hostilities. Even if the Fortress gunners appeared to be decimating the *Jagdflieger*, it became increasingly obvious that only fighter escort would reduce bomber losses. P-38 Lightnings were urgently required but, though promised, were long in coming. Meanwhile the Thunderbolt was proving that it was not the 'flying brick' many had judged it to be.

The obvious way to increase the P-47's range was the use of auxiliary, jettisonable fuel tanks, but here there was a significant problem. The reduction of atmospheric pressure as altitude increased meant that fuel would not draw properly from these tanks above 23,000ft. Pressurising the tanks was the answer, and the Eighth Air Force Air Technical Section devised a method of doing this by utilising the exhaust from the aircraft's instrument vacuum pump. Existing ferry tanks designed for the P-47 were not suitable as they were made of a plastic composition material, so the steel 75 US gallon capacity tanks as used on P-39s and P-40s were employed. Before the modifica-

**Right:** Reception party for the CO. On 15 May 1943 Canadian Squadron Leader Edward 'Jack' Charles, leading a section of No 611 Squadron Spitfire IXs, shot down two Fw 190s and Commandant R. Mouchotte of No 341 Squadron claimed another, for the 1,000th enemy aircraft claim by Biggin Hill sector squadrons. The action took place south-east of Caen and brought Charles his tenth and eleventh victories. He would ultimately gain 15° victory credits, three of which were obtained with the aircraft in the photograph, EN554/FY:Y. This Spitfire was missing in action with another squadron in September 1944. Both Wing Commander Alan Deere and Group Captain Malan flew with No 611 on the 15 May operation. (IWM CH9982)

**Right:** Typhoon IB DN249/HF:A of No 183 Squadron displays for the camera over Gatwick, April 1943. The black and white bands on the underwing surfaces was a recognition aid to discourage trigger-happy anti-aircraft gunners. Although markedly different in shape, the Typhoon was often mistaken for the Fw 190, although this may have been partially due to the engine noise, which was more akin to that of enemy raiders than the familiar Merlin note. There were also several incidents where 'friendly' fighter pilots mistook Typhoons for Focke-Wulfs and attacked. Despite training courses some individuals never developed an acumen for aircraft recognition. (IWM CH9292)

tions could be effected, a few missions were run half-filling the unpressurised 200 US gallon ferry tanks. The first sorties, on 28 July, took the Thunderbolts to the Dutch/German border where claims of nine enemy fighters were made. Two days later, after releasing the ferry tanks at the Dutch coast, the P-47s penetrated an additional 75 miles beyond their normal radius of action, undoubtedly surprising the *Luftwaffe* fighters, who did not expect to see American fighters so far inland. The Me 109s encountered were attacking a B-17 formation and the P-47 pilots claimed sixteen of them shot down, their highest claim so far.

*Luftwaffe* fighter pilots now faced a similar situation to that of RAF Fighter Command during the Battle of Britain. The principle objective for the British fighters had been the bomber

**Right:** During 1942 and 1943 Typhoons were used for intercepting the wave-hopping *Jabo* fighter-bombers that were so difficult to catch. The CO of No 195 Squadron, Squadron Leader D. M. Taylor, and his No 2 were flying a standing patrol from Ludham on 15 May 1943 when they saw a *Jabo* raid on Southwold. The No 2, Flight Sergeant Dickie Hough, shot down an Me 109G, only to have two cannon shells from the Messerschmitt's partner rip holes in the port wing and fuselage of his aircraft (DN389/JE:F). Such was the damage that the Typhoon was not deemed worthy of repair when he landed back at base. The line of small patches round the rear fuselage is a standard strengthening modification, although this did not completely cure the Typhoon's habit of shedding tail ends. This was No 195 Squadron's first and only air victory before disbandment in February 1944. Richard Hough became a noted biographer in postwar years. (IWM CE73)

formations, and in attacking these they themselves were exposed to being attacked from above. The Me 109s could usually catch the Hurricanes and Spitfires that attempted to evade by diving away. In this reversed situation, although the P-47's weight mitigated against good climb performance, in coming down, although initial acceleration was poor, it could out-dive most other fighters of its day. Moreover, the standard evasive tactic practised by Me 109 and Fw 190 pilots remained the 'split-S', half-roll and dive away under, which had proved successful time and time again in escaping from Spitfires. That this manoeuvre was not valid in evading P-47 interception at high altitudes was apparently not generally appreciated by the

*Jagdflieger* for some months as many of their pilots continued to attempt to escape attack in this way, only to experience the blast of eight 'point-fifties'.

The first use of the pressurised 75 US gallon 'belly tanks', so called because they were suspended from shackles on the underside of the P-47's fuselage, occurred in late August. The P-47 squadrons could now retain the auxiliary tanks until emptied or joining combat, keeping sufficient fuel in internal tanks for the return to England. With these tanks Thunderbolts were able to fly to Emden on 8 November 1943 to afford target cover for B-17s. Meanwhile Air Technical Section had arranged for the manufacture of steel 108 US gallon tanks in Britain. As

**Left:** De Havilland Mosquito IIs of No 605 Squadron, DZ716/UP:L leading and DZ724/UP:S on its wing, exhibit for the camera over East Anglia. A hundred miles per hour faster than the Beaufighter, the 'Wooden Wonder' was developed as the RAF's main night fighter from 1943. (IWM CH9474)

**Right:** Thunderbolts of the 334th Fighter Squadron gather for take-off at Debden in this view from the control tower, 15 May 1943. All returned from an uneventful sweep over the Netherlands. The *Luftwaffe Jagdgruppen* initially saw no great threat from the heavy US fighter and tended to ignore these intrusions, only intercepting if a favourable opportunity was presented. (USAAF)

sheet steel supplies were difficult to obtain, a pressurised paper/plastic tank of similar capacity was developed based on the type used for ferrying Hurricanes. Four more Thunderbolt groups arrived in England during the autumn of 1943, raising the number of these fighters in VIII Fighter Command to 500 and allowing a relay system of escort to be perfected. To make the most of fuel supplies a group formation would be detailed to fly directly to a pre-assigned part of the planned bomber route to take up escort.

Although the development of pressurised drop tanks proved successful in extending the Thunderbolt's range, by October 1943 the losses of VIII Bomber Command B-17s and B-24s exceeded 10 per cent on some missions, a figure that was deemed critical. What had been made plain in recent weeks was that where fighter escort was on hand the losses were much reduced. If the US daylight bomber campaign were to continue, it could only do so without prohibitive losses by long-range fighters accompanying the formations. To this end General Eaker finally received two groups of Lockeed P-38 Lightnings for, it was hoped, fighter support to be taken well into central Germany. It was found that the endurance of the P-38H was little better than the P-47 on internal fuel, so this model was soon withdrawn from operational service. The P-38J had provision for additional fuel tanks behind the wing leading edges and, when employing two 150 US gallon drop tanks, this model had a radius of action of 400 miles from England—a distance dictated by the amount of fuel it was necessary to retain in internal tanks for the return flight.

Enthusiasm for the P-38 was soon to wane when it was found that there was an acute problem with the low temperatures and humidity encountered at high altitude over north-west Europe. The hydraulic control lines of the turbo-superchargers froze, causing the units to fail; cockpit heating was so poor that pi-

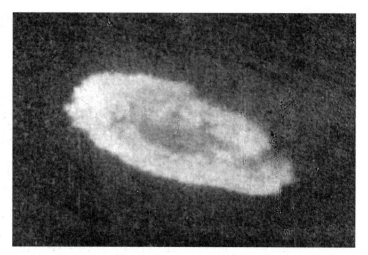

**Above:** The attacks on Coastal Command aircraft and those in transit to and from North Africa by *Luftwaffe* long-range fighters over the Bay of Biscay led Fighter Command to provide standing patrols by Beaufighters and Mosquitos during 1943. No 25 Squadron was involved during the summer, and on 11 June five Mosquito IIs met an equal number of *KG 40* Ju 88s. Flight Lieutenant Joe Singleton, flying DZ685, despatched one, the crew taking to their parachutes. The photograph shows the foaming ring in the sea where the Junkers struck. The previous January Singleton and his radar navigator, Flying Officer W. Haslem, claimed the first night raider that the squadron shot down with a Mosquito. (IWM C3651)

lots were in danger of suffering frostbite; and, worst of all, engine temperatures were so low that the Allisons often shed connecting rods. It is estimated that between October 1943 and March 1944 more P-38s were lost directly or indirectly to mechanical failure than to enemy action. Even with such handicaps the Lightning pilots were able to give the bombers some protection at long range, although the Fortresses and Liberators did not really get into their stride in hitting distant targets until the arrival of the fighter type that would provide the answer to the escort problem—the P-51B Mustang with the Packard Merlin engine.

**Left, upper:** In general, whenever possible the *Wehrmacht* gave dead Allied fliers a military funeral. This grave party at Moorsele on 2 June 1943 attended Lieutenant Pat Williams, a 63rd Fighter Squadron pilot, killed when his P-47 went out of control over the Low Countries, through, it is believed, Williams suffering anoxia. (NLV)

**Left, lower:** Lieutenant Ralph Johnson, in the cockpit of 62nd Fighter Squadron P-47D 42-7922, talks to Major David Schilling, his squadron CO. The flamboyant and highly popular Schilling later took command of the 56th Fighter Group. He had been credited with a total of $22\frac{1}{2}$ air victories when he finally moved from this famous organisation to an Eighth Air Force staff appointment early in 1945. The British Mk II reflector gun sight can be seen aft of the cockpit windshield below the rear-view mirror. The original N-3 model fitted in P-47s was often replaced by this superior type. (USAAF)

**Right:** A ground crew 'pull through' the engine of a P-47C to clear the cylinders of any accumulated fuel before start up. This 78th Fighter Group aircraft at Duxford carries a bulbous 200 US gallon ferry tank of the type which was used to extend range on a few missions during the summer of 1943. The triangular piece on the front of the tank was a wooden block installed so that air would force the tank off and clear when it was released in flight. (USAAF)

**Below:** Fighter pilots were encouraged to keep fit by indulging in sports. This volleyball net was set up not far from the Duxford control tower in the summer of 1943, the well-worn nature of the pitch indicating how popular the activity was. (USAAF)

**Right:** Accident was common in all air forces during the Second World War. On average six fighter aircraft were written off every day in Britain during the last two years of the war. Many fell out of the sky, hazarding civilian life. The weather deteriorated when a flight of 350th Fighter Squadron Thunderbolts flew from Metfield to Biggin Hill for GCI training on 5 September 1943. In heavy rain and low cloud two aircraft crashed, their pilots being killed. Lieutenant Irving Venell's LH:K hit a house. (USAAF)

**Right:** Douglas Bader and his physical handicap are legendary, but the RAF had a number of limbless aircrew. One of the most daring was Squadron Leader James MacLachlan, who had his left forearm amputated after being hit by a cannon shell from an Me 109 and forced to bale out of a Hurricane while flying in the defence of Malta. This was in February 1941, and he was back in the air by the autumn and commanding No 1 Squadron in November. Joining the Air Fighting Development Unit at Wittering, he was involved in experimental low-level sorties flying the Mustang IA, making his first operational sortie since being wounded on 29 June. With Flight Lieutenant Geoffrey Page, who had been shot down and badly injured during the Battle of Britain, flying as his No 2 in another Mustang, he encountered several enemy aircraft south of Paris. Four Hs 126s and two Ju 88s were despatched. The gun camera frames show MacLachlan's first Hs 126 going down and (bottom) one of the Ju 88s attacked. These claims took his total to $16^1/_2$ destroyed. On 18 July, during another sortie with the same Mustang, FD442, the engine caught fire and when 'bellying-in' in a French field the aircraft disintegrated. MacLachlan, critically injured, died in a German field hospital later that month. (IWM C3799A/C3805A)

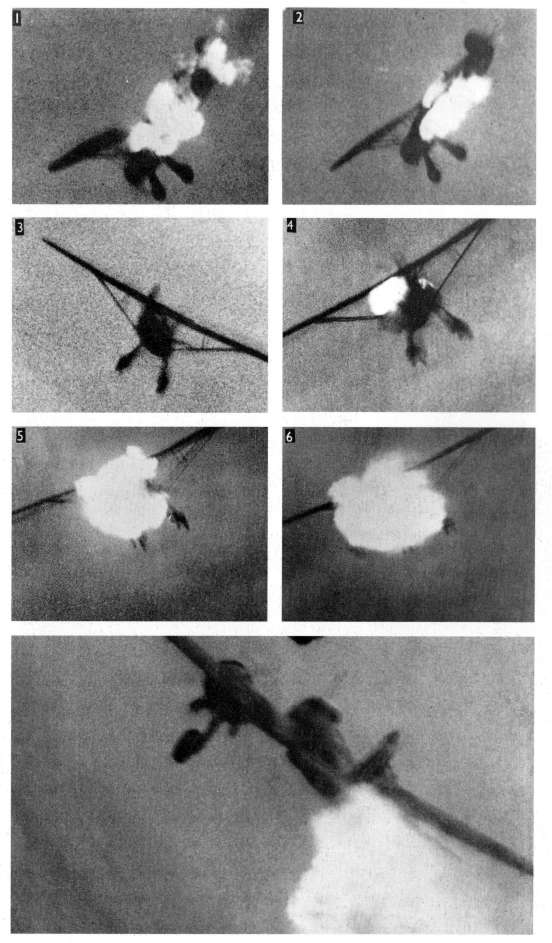

**Left:** The 40mm cannon was adapted as an air-to-ground weapon and installed on the trusty Hurricane. Some 300 Hurricane IIDs were produced and Nos 164 and 184 Squadrons were the only two in Britain to receive them. They were soon replaced by Hurricane IVs with the 'universal wing' which could also take the 40mm cannon. Known as the Vickers 'S' gun, with 15 rounds per magazine its slow rate of fire required high pilot skills to hit a target, usually enemy coastal shipping. Two .303 machine guns were retained and used with tracer rounds to aid target sighting. The 40mm weapon was eventually discarded in favour of the ground-to-air rocket. The 'S' gun in the photograph was on Hurricane IV KX413/FJ:H of No 164 Squadron at Middle Wallop in June 1943. (IWM CH10224)

**Left, upper:** An Me 109G under attack by Flight Sergeant Graham Shouldice of No 403 Squadron in July 1943. Five Messerschmitts were seen climbing to the same level as No 403 Squadron, 28,000ft, in the Abbeville area. The leader led an attack and in total three of the enemy aircraft were claimed. That shot down by Shouldice shed several pieces and appeared to have an engine explosion, and after an undercarriage leg extended the fighter went into a spin. On 17 August Shouldice collided with his CO's aircraft while manoeuvring to attack an Fw 190 at 26,000ft. Squadron Leader Walter Conrad's Spitfire had its fuselage severed, but the pilot managed to bale out and evade capture. Shouldice was not so fortunate: he and his damaged Spitfire disappeared into the Channel while trying to regain England. (IWM C3655)

**Left, lower:** The top-ranking RAF fighter pilot in claims of enemy aircraft in western Europe was J. E. ('Johnnie') Johnson, who was credited with 34 destroyed and seven shared, plus several probably destroyed and damaged. At the time this was reckoned to be his 20th enemy aircraft, which he shot down while leading the Canadian Wing he commanded during a sweep near Oisement on 15 July 1943. He was flying his personal Spitfire IX EN398/JE:J, in which at least sixteen of his victories were made. (IWM C3667)

**Right:** An RAF Fighter Command wing was usually centred on one main sector airfield controlling three or four squadrons currently assigned to that sector. The first Australian airman to command a fighter wing in Britain was Wing Commander John R. Ratten, who had previously been CO of No 453 Squadron. In his new position he continued to fly Spitfire IX EN522/FU:F, which carried his wife's nickname *Tikkie*. EN522 was wrecked in a flying accident while serving with another squadron on 28 July 1944. (IWM CH10048)

**Above:** Some RAF squadrons still preferred to operate in flights of three as late as the summer of 1943. These are Spitfire IXs of No 222 Squadron over Newchurch, early October 1943.

The Spitfire Vs parked on the far side of the airfield are those of No 132 Squadron, which was based at Newchurch at this time. (IWM 11473)

**Below:** During a 'Circus' operation on 15 August 1943 No 266 Squadron Typhoons were bounced by Fw 190s in the Guipavas area. Three Typhoons were shot down, including that of Squadron Leader A. S. Macintyre, the CO. Flight Sergeant Derek Erasmus, a 20-year-old Rhodesian, described the action. 'We were in three sections of two when four Fw 190s dived down on us. Four more of the tribe sat up top in the sun, waiting to pick us off. We turned into the four that came down and a general dogfight followed. I saw one of them firing at one of my pals. As he broke away I closed with him. Once I had got him nicely in my sights, I went right in, pressing my gun button all the way, and he blew up just in front of my nose.' The Fw 190A that Erasmus destroyed was that which had shot down his CO. Erasmus was commissioned later in the year and eventually rose to Squadron Leader and command of No 193 Squadron. After some 200 hours of operational flying in Typhoons he lost his life in March 1945. It is believed that debris from the ground target he was attacking brought down his Typhoon. (IWM C3847)

**Below:** Strafing armed vessels was a particularly hazardous business as the defences usually had an open field of fire devoid of obstructions. On 27 September 1943 Typhoons of No 198 Squadron, attacking a barge convoy in the entrance to the Masgat, came under intensive fire from three naval auxiliaries. Two aircraft were hit badly and their pilots baled out, while 22-year-old Squadron Leader J. M. Bryan, the CO, sustained a hit in the ammunition compartment of his starboard wing. The detonation also exploded some 20mm rounds, rending a 2ft wide hole in the wing and causing such a loss of lift that 'Mike' Bryan had to use both hands and a leg to keep the stick well over. As the aircraft was coming into land at Manston, the wing suddenly dipped at 140mph, causing JP666/TP:N to go down hard on the right wheel and career off at 40 degrees to the runway with the right wing-tip scraping the turf until the speed dropped and the left wing came down. One of the most distinguished of Typhoon commanders, with a record of causing serious damage to over 50 enemy vessels in strafing and rocket attacks, Bryan lost his life flying with another squadron early in the Normandy campaign the following year. (IWM CE108)

**Right:** Lightnings finally arrived in Britain during August 1943 to provide escort for Eighth Air Force bombers. Their introduction into operations was delayed by equipment modifications. Unfortunately the P-38 did not live up to its promise as a high-altitude fighter due chiefly to the extreme cold having an adverse effect on engines. It did not lack in armament and was considered an excellent gun platform as all weapons were mounted in the nose. The lifted hood reveals the tray magazines for the .50-calibre machine guns and the large drum holding the 20mm rounds for the centrally mounted cannon. (USAAF)

One of seven new squadrons formed to fly Typhoons at the end of 1942, No 193 would use only this type during its 32-month existence. It became the second 'Fellowship of the Bellows' squadron, this generous Brazilian association 'presenting' funds for nine new Typhoons in the autumn of 1943, here in line for inspection at Harrowbeer in October. The nearest aircraft, JP919/DP:X, would be lost to flak near Malmédy on Christmas Eve 1944, the pilot from No 168 Squadron being taken prisoner. Next in line is JP918, which came to grief the next day when force-landed in the same area by a No 168 Squadron pilot owing to fuel failure. Fighter aircraft frequently taken out of service for repair, overhaul or modification rarely returned to the same unit. (IWM CH11393)

**Above:** Distinctive shapes: P-38H Lightnings of the 20th Fighter Group fly over their Kingscliffe base, October 1943. (USAAF)

**Left:** T/Sgts James Lane (left) and Joe Taglov fix a 150 US gallon drop tank to the pylon of P-38H 42-67067 of the 20th Fighter Group at Kingscliffe, October 1943. The P-38H was soon withdrawn from operations as its internal fuel storage only permitted a maximum radius of action of 300 miles. A shortage of P-38s kept the 20th Fighter Group from full operational commitment until the end of the year. (USAAF)

**Above:** Lieutenant-Colonel Loren McCollom, CO of the 353rd Fighter Group, briefs his pilots for a practice mission from Metfield, October 1943. McCollom was shot down the following month to spend the rest of the war as a prisoner. His successor, Glenn Duncan (second left in the back row) was shot down the following spring but evaded capture. Two other commanders of this group were killed, one in combat, the other in an accident. The pilot on the extreme left, front row, is making notes of essential details on the back of his hand in ink, a common practice with fighter pilots. (USAAF)

**Right:** Corporal Michael Senia installs a film in the gun camera of a 353rd Fighter Group P-47D. The 16mm unit operated automatically when the guns were fired to record strikes or otherwise. By 1943 gun cameras were a standard installation in all Allied front-line fighter aircraft, providing evidence to confirm or dismiss pilot's claims. However, assessment of exposed gun camera film was often faulty: an aircraft that appeared doomed did not always crash. (USAAF)

**Left:** Flying Officer Ralph Hofer, a one-time volunteer for the RAF who shot down an Me 109 on his first combat mission on 8 October 1943, poses in P-47D 42-7945/QP:D at Debden. The irrepressible 'Kid' Hofer was to excel when the 4th Fighter Group converted to P-51Bs the following February but was often cautioned about engaging enemy aircraft without his Flight Leader's permission. He had run up a score of 15 enemy aircraft shot down by 2 July 1944 when, on a sweep over the Balkans flown from Italy, he was last seen climbing towards enemy fighters. The only high-scoring USAAF pilot to die as a result of air combat, it is believed that he was shot down by one of the *Luftwaffe*'s *Experten*. (USAAF)

**Below:** Thunderbolts of the 82nd Fighter Squadron lined up for a four-a-time take-off at Duxford. Each section would be rapidly followed by the next, so that the whole squadron would be airborne in under a minute. This was possible as Duxford had no concrete runways until early 1945. (USAAF)

**Above:** On 26 November 1943 the 56th Fighter Group decimated formations of Me 110s and Me 410s preparing to attack Eighth Air Force bombers near Oldenburg. The group made claims of 18 destroyed plus five of the Me 109s that were giving the *Zerstörergruppen* top cover. Relaxing back in the interrogation room at Halesworth, Captain Walker 'Bud' Mahurin (second left), who shot down three Me 110s, discusses the mission with Lieutenant Harold 'Bunny' Comstock, another victor, enjoying a smoke and a sandwich. The other two 63rd Fighter Squadron pilots are Lieutenants Raymond Petty and Fred Windmayer, wingmen who did not have an opportunity to score. On the next mission, three days later, Windmayer (far left) failed to return. (USAAF)

**Right:** Another victor on 26 November was Major Francis Gabreski, who shot down two Me 110s. On return to Halesworth his crew chief discovered an unexploded 20mm round lodged in the Thunderbolt's engine. Had the missile exploded Gabreski might not have gone on to destroy a total of 28 *Luftwaffe* aircraft and five enemy jets over Korea in air combat, to become one of most distinguished of all American fighter pilots. Looking at the missile which 'Gabby' is holding is the 61st Fighter Squadron flight surgeon, Captain George Horning. (USAAF)

**Below:** The European winter weather contributed to the deaths of many fighter pilots. Squadrons were at times despatched on missions in reasonable conditions only to find fog or a 'solid undercast' on return. On 11 December 1943 P-47 pilots of the 355th Fighter Group found visibility severely reduced by mists on reaching their home base, Steeple Morden. Lieutenant Jack Woertz apparently thought he would overshoot on his approach when seeing the runway. His aircraft was seen to stall and crash into a field of brussels sprouts, the impact completely severing the tail section. The pilot was killed. (USAAF)

**Above:** Bad weather was also partly to blame for another crash on 16 December 1943 when the 355th Fighter Group flew escort to Bremen. Low on fuel, many of the group's P-47s landed away from home station. While orbiting Rackheath Lieutenant Harold Macrudy's Thunderbolt, 42-8689, ran out of fuel and he was obliged to make a dead-stick landing. Unfortunately he overran on to ploughed land, the main landing gear sank in and the aircraft flipped over on its back. However, Macrudy was extracted unhurt. The following month, after claiming two Me 109s, he was promptly shot down by another. Evading capture, he was befriended by the French Resistance and stayed with them until the summer of 1944. (USAAF)

**Below:** The majority of fighter-versus-fighter interceptions were from the rear and armour plate was provided to protect the pilot. On the Spitfire this was $2\frac{1}{2}$in (6.2mm) thick behind his head and $1\frac{3}{4}$in (4.5mm) behind his back, sufficient to withstand a 30mm hit. Flight Lieutenant Arthur Sager had personal experience of this during a sweep off the Dutch coast in November 1943. He was in combat with Me 109Gs when a 30mm shell detonated just behind his seat, destroying the radio and perforating adjacent areas of the fuselage. The cockpit filled with smoke and momentarily Sager thought his engine was on fire. The only hurt to Sager was a splitting headache, which did not stop him landing the No 416 Squadron Spitfire safely at base. (IWM CE110)

**Above:** The first Merlin-engine Mustangs commenced operations from Boxted in December 1943. During the next few weeks technical and operational problems became evident, but it was clear that the Mustang was the answer to the USAAF's long-range escort problem. The determining factor was having sufficient integral tankage fuel to enter combat and return to base once drop tanks had been released. The tactical radius of the P-47D and P-38J at this time was 300 and 450 miles respectively; the P-51B's was 650 with two 75 US gallon drop tanks as illustrated. The P-51B in the foreground, 43-12173/GQ:A, was Major George Bickell's aircraft. Later in December 1943 the Mustangs donned white identification bands over wings and nose surfaces for identification purposes: the idea that any single-engine monoplane with square-cut wing-tips must be an Me 109 persisted, despite the fact that the 109E had long gone from *Luftwaffe* fighter *Staffeln*. (USAAF)

**Left:** The three squadron commanders of the 354th Fighter Group's P-51Bs had seen service against the Japanese. Thirty-year-old Major James Howard, left, CO of the 356th Fighter Squadron, had flown with the American Volunteer Group in China and Burma. Major George Bickell, centre, CO of the 355th Fighter Squadron, and Major Owen Seaman, CO of the 353rd Fighter Squadron, had both been in Hawaii at the time of the attack on Pearl Harbor. Howard was to win the only Medal of Honor to be awarded to a pilot for fighter action over Europe, and Bickell eventually became the 354th Group's commander. Seaman was lost in the North Sea on 16 December, the day after this photograph was taken at Boxted. His squadron would end the war with a higher score of enemy aircraft destroyed in air combat, 290, than any other USAAF squadron in all war theatres. (USAAF)

**Right:** It was not unknown for fighter pilots inadvertently to shoot down one of their comrades during combat. This usually occurred when two pilots were firing at the same target and one aircraft passed in front of the other. On 22 December 1943 the 352nd Fighter Group encountered a number of twin-engine enemy fighters in the Zwolle area. Major Everett Stewart dived on an Me 110 but a fraction of a second after he had fired another member of his flight, Lieutenant John Coleman, attacked the same aircraft. Stewart's gun camera recorded Coleman's attack, one of the few air fighting photographs where both assailant and victim can be seen. The dark haze around the P-47's wings is gun smoke. The white blotch on the Me 110's wing is where it is being hit. (USAAF)

**Below:** On 30 December 1943 a Ju 52/3m fitted with a degaussing ring was minesweeping low over the sea a few miles off the French Atlantic coast near the approaches to the U-boat base at Lorient. The location was some 200 miles from the nearest British fighter base, and there were reasonable grounds for considering such vulnerable aircraft safe from attack while performing this work. Unfortunately for the crew their course crossed that of a formation of No 266 Squadron Typhoons on a long-range sweep. Flying Officer N. J. Lucas in ZH:D and Flying Officer W. V. Mollett in ZH:L were ordered to attack. The gun camera pictures are from the aircraft flown by Mollett, who later described the action: 'The Junkers turned to starboard and my colleague, Flying Officer Lucas, got in bursts which set both engines on fire. Then I went in and as I broke away I saw half the fuselage and one wing burning. Then the enemy crashed into the sea. We could see no survivors.' (IWM C4095A)

**Below:** Squadron Leader M. P. C. Holmes poses in front of his Typhoon IB JP504/OV:Z with pet dog Ace, Tangmere, October 1943. Both pilot and machine would be missing in action. When flying another Typhoon the popular 'Jacko' Holmes of No 197 Squadron was seen to have an engine fire and, out of control, crash near Buchey, France, on 24 January 1944. It is not known if this was due to enemy action. After modifications his original Typhoon, JP504, issued to No 137 Squadron, was shot down by flak near St Vith on 26 December 1944, the pilot being killed. (IWM CH11584)

**Right:** Various surfaces were tried on some of the Advanced Landing Grounds being prepared in Kent for air support of the forthcoming cross-Channel invasion. At Ashford a prefabricated bituminous covering was laid and tested with different tactical aircraft. This is a No 174 Squadron Typhoon, XP:M, landing on 21 October 1943. The chief problem was that of rainwater building up into sizeable puddles in low areas. (USAAF)

Below: The shackles that held an auxiliary fuel tank to the belly of a Thunderbolt could also be used to hold a bomb. When weather reduced the frequency of heavy bomber raids and consequently the need for escort, VIII Fighter Command experimented with fighter-bomber operations. The 353rd Fighter Group at Metfield was foremost in these activities, trying different methods of attack. Here M/Sgt Clarence Riffer watches Sergeant Tom Zetterval fix the fin assembly to a 500lb HE bomb while Corporal Dave Winner holds the jack trolley. The P-47D is 42-8602/YJ:E of the 351st Fighter Squadron. (USAAF)

# 11
# AIR SUPERIORITY IN HOSTILE AIRSPACE

Surprisingly, the initial production mark of the Packard Merlin-engine Mustang was not seen as a long-range air superiority fighter. The USAAF had followed the RAF in employing the Allison engine version chiefly for tactical reconnaissance and ground attack, even developing a dive-bombing model, and Materiel Command expected the Merlin Mustang, the P-51B, to fill a similar role. To this end the first production P-51Bs were sent to the US Ninth Air Force in England, the tactical organisation forming to support the cross-Channel invasion of continental Europe. This can be partly explained by the Eighth Air Force's confidence that the P-38 Lightning would fulfil any long-range escort requirement and was quite able to take on the opposition. In this its commanders were undoubtedly influenced by the Air Technical Section, which was led by a strong pro-P-38 lobby. Experience with the Lightnings that began operations from England in the autumn of 1943 quickly made it clear to even the most ardent P-38 enthusiast that this aircraft was not living up to expectations. There were already those who saw the potential of the Mustang as a long-range fighter, most notably Tommy Hitchcock, the Air Attaché of the US Embassy in London, who had keenly supported the British in seeking US production of a Merlin-powered model after flying a Rolls-Royce conversion in England.

**Below:** Mud, mud, nothing but mud. Leiston, the only new airfield built to Class A specification for fighter use was initially home to the 358th Fighter Group, which became operational on 20 December 1943. A P-47D of its 367th Fighter Squadron stands ready on a concrete pad amidst the mire of a base still in the final stages of construction: a view towards the technical site from the control tower. The 358th was not long with the Eighth Air Force, being exchanged for a much-needed Mustang group, the 357th, at the end of January 1944. (M. Olmsted Collection)

The first Ninth Air Force P-51B group became operational on 1 December 1943, initially under the control of VIII Fighter Command. To give the fighter even greater range 75 US gallon jettisonable tanks could be carried under each wing, and an additional 85 US gallon fuel tank was installed in the fuselage behind the cockpit. Like all new models, the P-51B had technical problems, in this case coolant leaks, oil throwing at the propeller hub and windshield frosting. More critical was the replacement of engine mounting bolts and the jamming of three of the four wing-mounted .50-calibre machine guns if fired when exposed to excessive gravitational forces. The latter was due to the canted positioning of the guns relative to the ammunition feed, and the remedy was electrical booster motors on the trace to overcome the G forces. Despite these problems it was quickly evident that the Merlin Mustang was the escort fighter the Eighth Air Force sought. For the first time fighter cover could be given over any target the bombers were likely to attack and efforts were in hand to wrest the Mustangs from assignment to the Ninth Air Force. Agreement was reached that two of the four groups scheduled to be equipped with the P-51B on arrival in England would be exchanged for P-47 groups and the remaining two would continue under VIII Fighter Command's operational control until the following spring. Moreover, for the time being, the Eighth Air Force would have priority in P-51B production and it was planned to convert several P-47 groups to the type as soon as possible.

The first P-51B group was not joined by a second until February 1944 and a third and fourth at the end of that month, one of which had converted from P-47s. Although this placed some 200 Mustangs on operational status and allowed fighter cover over Berlin for the first Eighth Air Force bombing of the enemy capital in March, up to that time it was primarily the P-47 Thunderbolts that provided the main long-range escort force for the American heavy bombers. By the beginning of February 1944 the Eighth Air Force had nine P-47 groups (27 squadrons) operational and the Ninth Air Force had three under VIII Fighter Command's operational control, while there were still only two P-38 groups and the solitary P-51B group. This force amounted to nearly a thousand fighters, and with RAF Fighter Command the *Luftwaffe*, in spite of having built up its fighter strength in the west to 870 single-engine and 780 twin-engine aircraft, was overwhelmed in areas lying within 250 miles of south-east England. Many *Jagdgruppen* were now based within the *Reich*, and most of the twin-engine aircraft were night fighters. But it was not just force of numbers that brought an ever-worsening attrition to the German fighters.

By avoiding contact with the P-47 support to concentrate on the B-17s and B-24s during the summer and autumn of 1943, the *Jagdflieger* had allowed the American pilots to gain experience and develop tactics. From high summer and through the winter of 1943/44 one of the original Thunderbolt groups had been unusually successful in air combat, at one point having in total one hundred claims more than any other US fighter group. The same group promoted a competitive spirit among

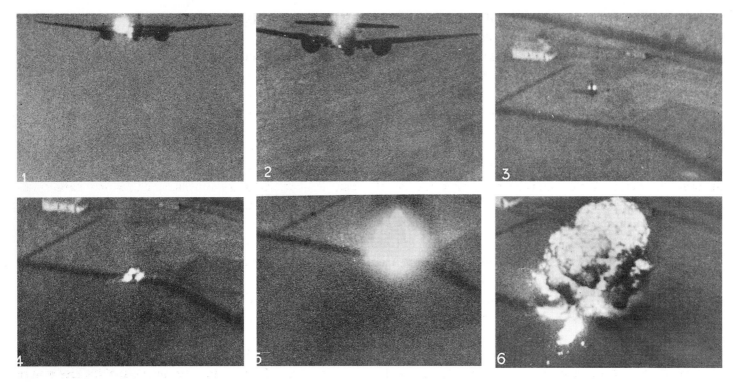

**Above:** Night and bad-weather intruder operations meant that there could never be a safe area for the *Luftwaffe* within 400 miles of the United Kingdom. Clermont Ferrand airfield was generally a quiet haven far removed from the Allied air forces' attention—but not on 27 January 1944, when Mosquito VIs of the Canadian No 418 Squadron arrived in the area. Probably the first thing the unfortunate crew of this Ju 88 knew of the attack was that they were being blasted out of the sky by cannon shells. Flying Officer Johnny Caine came upon the Junkers near the airfield at about 50ft and gave a three-second burst. Caine also shot down Ju W.34s on this sortie and in the following weeks was particularly successful in strafing aircraft on land or water. By the end of hostilities his 'score' stood at 20 enemy aircraft destroyed, 15 of which were on their bases. (IWM C4153A)

other fighter groups for the leadership in the total of enemy aircraft shot down. This was encouraged by VIII Fighter Command to the extent of issuing press releases identifying individual groups by their CO's name. Moreover, this built up an aggressive morale among the American fighter units.

The success of the leading Thunderbolt group came partly through good air discipline and tactics. VIII Fighter Command had first followed the practices of the RAF in providing close escort for bomber formations, but the leaders of this group realised that the most advantageous way to afford the bombers protection would be to break up the *Luftwaffe* fighter assemblies when they were forming to attack. To this end part of a P-47 formation was sent ahead and often took the Me 109 and Fw 190 *Gruppen* by surprise. Another reason for the high totals of claims was because pilots were allowed to continue to pursue enemy aircraft when they dived away; as described previously, the evasive tactic that had worked so well against Spitfires could be fatal if tried with a following Thunderbolt. Soon these same tactics were common to all US P-47 groups and they were primarily responsible for advancing the demise

of the *Jagdflieger*. Many of the great *Experten*—such as Philipp, Mayer and Rall—were brought down by P-47 pilots.

Additionally, in January 1944 VIII Fighter Command permitted formations that had finished their bomber support or escort assignment to go down and strafe enemy airfields, so that the *Luftwaffe* had no sanctuary on the ground. The strafing was extended to communications targets, notably rail traffic. Ground attack would quickly prove more dangerous for the US fighters than aerial combat, particularly at airfields, where they were usually subjected to heavy concentrations of light flak and machine-gun fire. To find the most prudent method of conducting strafing attacks on well-defended targets, VIII Fighter Command set up a provisional squadron to carry out operational experiments.

If the P-47 groups had shown the way, they were still limited in radius of action to some 300 miles from home base, even with the larger 108 and 150 US gallon drop tanks introduced during the winter of 1943/44. The limiting factor of their range was retaining enough internally carried fuel for return to base once the auxiliary tanks had been dropped. From March 1944 it was the Mustang pilots that made the headlines, being responsible for most of the enemy fighters claimed in combat. During the first major American raid on Berlin, on 6 March 1944, which developed into one of the biggest air battles of the war, 81 enemy aircraft were claimed shot down by the seventeen VIII and IX Fighter Command fighter groups participating. Of these claims, two were by P-38s, 38 by P-47s and 41 by P-51s, although only 100 P-51s were despatched as against 615 P-47s—and this achievement was at the cost of only one P-38 and five each P-47s and P-51s. The inevitable overclaiming occurred as the true total of *Luftwaffe* losses in combat was 66, including at least half a dozen brought down by bomber gunners' fire. Even so, it was a 5-to-1 showing in favour of the US fighters, and the ever-mounting daylight raids would continue to have similar outcomes. The P-51B excelled, not only because of its endurance, but because of its speed, which was equal to or better than that of its opponents, and its diving ability. In fact the P-51B could outdive any other fighter type in service, including the P-47, enabling it to outrun an attacker and overtake a quarry, giving it the same position of superiority that had been held by the Me 109E during the Battle of Britain. This ability had been attained through advanced aerodynamic features.

If the totals of enemy aircraft shot down were exaggerated, they nevertheless gave an indication of the attrition suffered by the *Jagdflieger* as the claims for fourteen major missions to targets in the *Reich* flown between 8 March and 30 May show: 79, 77, 36, 44, 88, 51, 42, 34, 57, 55, 61, 70, 39 and 50. Indeed, the *Luftwaffe* had lost air superiority wherever the USAAF wished to venture. By the end of May 1944 the *Luftwaffe* not only had to contend with 600 Mustangs of the Eighth and Ninth Air Forces, but some 150 flying in support of the Fifteenth Air Force bombers based in southern Italy. The RAF had three squadrons equipped with the Mustang III, as the P-51B was called in that service, and although these did on occasion support the US heavy bomber raids they did not have the rear fuselage fuel tank installed and therefore had less endurance.

The voluntary ground strafing of enemy airfields by USAAF fighters, after completing an escort assignment, was adjudged so fruitful that dedicated large-scale strafing missions were planned. Under the code-name 'Jackpot', these were to be staged on days when poor weather prevented heavy bomber operations. Each fighter group was assigned a specified area of north-west or central Germany in which it alone would operate. This allowed pilots to become familiar with the airfields and defences in their domain and be in a better position to plan attack tactics. It was also designed to prevent overlapping, with a group arriving at an airfield already strafed by another unit and thus having its defences alerted. The first 'Jackpot' was flown on 15 April with 616 Lightnings, Thunderbolts and Mustangs despatched. Claims of eighteen enemy aircraft encountered in the air and 40 destroyed on the ground was not a particularly satisfactory outcome when balanced against 33 fighters failing to return and another two written off in crashes in Britain. However, nineteen of the losses were put down to the appalling weather—persistent low cloud, mist and rain. As nearly half the day's losses were the still precious Mustangs, there were some misgivings in higher command about committing fighters to long-range strafing missions in conditions where unbroken cloud rose to over 24,000ft. Nonetheless, a similar scheme for ground attack was planned against

**Right:** The Typhoons had a good day on 30 January 1944, claiming twelve enemy aircraft shot down for no losses in combats over northern France. No 198 Squadron was responsible for nine of these claims, and it is known that *JG 2* had six pilots killed this day. Led by Squadron Leader John Baldwin, they bounced a formation of Fw 190s between Rouen and La Roche. Flight Sergeant Ronald Crouch shot down one Focke-Wulf and claimed another as a probable, but his Typhoon, JR512/TP:J, took a cannon shell in the tail. Both pilot and this aircraft were victims of ground fire on 14 June the same year: Crouch was shot down in another Typhoon near Montebourg and JR512 crash-landed near Carentan, its pilot being safe. John Baldwin had 15 credited air victories during the Second World War and was lost while flying F-86 Sabres with the USAF in Korea in 1952. It is possible that he was accidentally shot down by his wingman in a combat with MiG-15s. (IWM CH12230)

communication systems, primarily rail traffic. The first of these so-called 'Chattanooga' strafing forays took place in less trying weather on 21 May. Of 617 fighters despatched, 27 failed to return, although the claims were impressive and included attacks on 225 locomotives, of which 91 were rated destroyed, 83 aircraft destroyed on airfields and 20 aircraft shot down, plus attacks on several other ground targets. There is little doubt that this operation caused much disruption, even allowing for optimistic assessment on the American side. Steam locomotives were not destroyed by 'fifty-calibre' bullets; but they were extensively damaged, and most, if not all, needed repair.

The losses again emphasised the dangers of ground strafing, the more so with the Germans alerted to such attacks and bolstering their defences around likely targets. Several commanding officers and leading aces had been lost to ground fire since ground attack had become a frequent activity of the USAAF fighters. There was nothing new in shooting up one's opponents aircraft at his home base—it had been practised during the First World War—but the Eighth Air Force had now gone far beyond that occasional activity: the fighter was being used as an offensive weapon on an unprecedented scale.

**Left:** P-51B 43-12216/AJ:U of the 356th Fighter Squadron, 354th Fighter Group, above a 'solid' undercast. Vast cloud masses are common during the northern European winter months. One of the remarkable aspects of Eighth Air Force long-range escort was the few navigational losses of single-seat fighters. In such circumstances as that depicted, a pilot had only the aid of a radioed request for a bearing to direct him home to England, perhaps from more than 300 miles. (USAF)

**Below left:** Lieutenant James Duffy of the 354th Fighter Squadron was a lucky man on 11 February 1944. On a bomber support mission at 27,000ft his oxygen system failed, causing him to black out and his P-47 to enter a dive. Duffy came to at around 4,000ft and brought the fighter under control. Deciding to hedge-hop home, he was unfortunate enough to encounter a light flak battery near Antwerp which put four 20mm shells into his P-47's nose, wing and tail. Duffy was not aware of the extent of the damage until he reached home base, Steeple Morden. The hole in the elevator suggests that P-47D 42-74681/WR:Y passed directly over the flak site. (USAAF)

**Above:** Captain Don Gentile, a pilot of No 121 'Eagle' Squadron who transferred to the USAAF, poses beside the scoreboard of the successor unit, the 335th Fighter Squadron, on 10 April 1944. At this time Gentile received publicity as the first US pilot in the Second World War to exceed First World War American ace Eddie Rickenbacker's 'score' of 26 enemy aircraft, but Gentile's 27 included six aircraft destroyed while ground strafing. Two of his 21 destroyed and two shared air victories were with the RAF. Gentile was killed in a flying accident post-war. (USAAF)

**Left:** Gentile's wingman in many of his combats was Lieutenant John Godfrey, here seen with his crew chief Sergeant Larry Krantz on P-51B 43-6765/VF:P. This Mustang, displaying Godfrey's eleven victory symbols, had a band of red and white checks under the exhaust manifold, as did Gentile's, personal markings for in-flight recognition which higher headquarters later ordered to be removed. Godfrey flew two tours, and his 18 air victories was the highest total for a 4th Fighter Group pilot. He was also credited with 12 strafing victories. (G. H. Weckbacker)

**Left:** 'He never knew what hit him.' An illustration of the fact that a great many pilots had no idea they were being attacked until their aircraft was hit: a burst from the eight 'point-fifties' of a P-47 results in a smoking engine, a gaping hole in the wing and an extending undercarriage leg. On 22 February 1944 Lieutenant-Colonel Glenn Duncan, CO of the 353rd Fighter Group, saw an Fw 190 cruising on a straight course at low altitude. The *Luftwaffe* aircraft continued on its way as Duncan's P-47 closed to about 75yds before firing. (USAAF)

**Right, upper:** In the summer of 1941 No 112 Squadron began conversion to the Curtiss Tomahawk at Fayid in the Middle East. The type's radiator inlet scoop below the nose gave it a rather shark-like appearance, which led to a decoration that became an unofficial squadron marking. Such embellishments were not approved of by British commands, yet when the Tomahawks of No 1686 Bomber Defence Training Flight at Hixton appeared with 'shark noses' they were apparently permitted. This example was seen on a visitor to Prestwick on 17 March 1944. (IWM CH18750)

**Right, lower:** Beaufighter storeyard. By the spring of 1944 Mosquitos had replaced Beaufighters in all but two of the United Kingdom-based night fighter squadrons, and these also converted to the more nimble de Havilland that summer. Here Beaufighter Mk VIFs withdrawn from operational service await disposal beside a line of ex-No 515 Squadron Merlin-powered Mk IIs. The Beaufighter IVs have AI Mk IV and V radars. (IWM CH16511)

**Left:** Wing Commander Keith M. Hampshire and his radar navigator Flying Officer T. Condon, both Australians, examining the wreckage of Ju 88 3E+AP of *KG 6* shot down at Walberton on the night of 24/25 March 1944. Hampshire commanded the only RAAF night fighter squadron, No 456, and before coming to Britain in the autumn of 1943 had seen service with Hudsons and Bostons operating against Japanese forces in New Guinea. In eleven weeks Hampshire and Condon destroyed seven *Luftwaffe* aircraft at night, all while flying Mosquito XVII HK286/RX:A. Ju 88 3E+AP was their first. (IWM CH12583)

**Below:** During a 'Baby Blitz' raid on London on 24/25 March 1944 one of the raiders was destroyed by Flying Officer Edward Hedgecoe and his radar navigator Flying Officer N. L. Bamford. Hedgecoe's account ran as follows: 'The Hun was weaving violently when we first saw him and we closed in to make sure he was a Ju 188. Then I fired. The result was a great explosion, and sheets of

blazing oil and masses of debris poured back over the Mosquito. In a few seconds our aircraft was ablaze from end to end. The cockpit cover was blackened with soot and I had to open the side panel and wipe clear a small patch through which to peer. We got down safely but the poor Mossie was scorched all over and the rudder almost burnt away.' Mosquito XVII VY:O with the new AI Mk X radar would never fly again. Hedgecoe was killed in a bad-weather accident in January 1945. (IWM CE136)

**Right:** The top-scoring pilot with twin-engine aircraft was Wing Commander John Braham, who had 29 destroyed and two probables to his credit before being shot down over the coast of Denmark and made prisoner in June 1944. Twenty of his victories were achieved as a night fighter pilot with Beaufighters, flying with Nos 29 and 141 Squadrons. He was then posted to No 2 Group headquarters but continued to fly on operations as opportunity allowed. These were with the group's Mosquito VI-equipped squadrons and included low-level fighter-bomber raids and 'Ranger' sorties flown to Norway and Denmark. On one occasion his Mosquito was so badly shot up by an enemy fighter that Braham had to ditch off the Norfolk coast. It was on another of

these sorties that he was eventually shot down. He is seen here in the cockpit of a Mosquito at Benson on 19 May 1944 with Flight Lieutenant W. J. Gregory, who was his radar operator for most of his successful night fighter claims. (IWM CH13176)

**Below:** An AI Mk VIIIB radar installation in a Mosquito XIII night fighter. The visor to keep outside light from the screen of the indicator unit is in place. This was hinged to swing back below the indicator unit

to allow easy access to the cockpit seating. Later marks of Mosquito night fighters were also fitted with a Lucerno unit as part of the instrument blind approach equipment for landing in darkness or bad weather. (IWM CH16607)

# 12
# FIGHTERS FOR 'OVERLORD'

**R**AF Spitfire squadrons had given effective fighter cover for Martin B-26 Marauder missions from the time these medium bombers began operating in strength from English bases, in the late summer of 1943. Indeed, the Marauder crews considered that their having the lowest loss rate per sortie of any Allied bomber was due in good part to the excellence of the Spitfire escort. Only in the latter half of 1943 was the supply of Spitfire IXs sufficient to convert the remaining squadrons equipped with the ageing and slower Mk V. The first Spitfires with the new Rolls-Royce Griffon engine, Mk XIIs, were brought into service during the spring of 1944. Only two squadrons used this mark, which had a good turn of speed at low altitude and was used for chasing Focke-Wulf *Jabos*. An upsurge in *Luftwaffe* night activity over Britain, which became known as the 'Little Blitz', took place during the first five months of 1944. London, again the main target, sometimes suffered up to 300 bomber sorties nightly, mainly by Do 217s. A very low-level approach across the Channel to avoid radar detection, a climb to higher altitude before bombing, followed by a tree- and wave-hopping withdrawal was the usual tactic. Even so, the scope of both ground and airborne tracking radar had been greatly improved and Mosquitos destroyed many of the raiders. A total of 253 aircraft were lost to the British defences by the *Luftwaffe* units involved—5.5 per cent of sorties.

As already stated, the cross-Channel invasion, code-named 'Overlord', was planned for the following spring. In June 1943 the RAF's tactical units had been brought together under a new command, the 2nd Tactical Air Force. Fighter Command was redesignated Air Defence of Great Britain and lost the larger part of its force to the 2nd Tactical Air Force. Army Cooperation Command was disbanded and its squadrons also came under the new command, as did those medium and light bomber squadrons of No 2 Group Bomber Command. With a mission to support British and Commonwealth ground forces, the 2nd Tactical Air Force was eventually composed of two groups of ground support fighters and one for air defence.

(An RAF group was equivalent to a USAAF tactical air command.) The hitherto disappointing Typhoon was developed as the principal British fighter-bomber and ground attack aircraft. In addition to working with 500lb and 1,000lb bombs, its power and sturdy wing made it a good vehicle for the air-to-ground rocket missile with a 60lb warhead, eight of these being carried. Spitfires with an underfuselage rack, originally developed for a jettisonable fuel tank, were able to deliver a 250lb or 500lb bomb.

The American contingent for 'Overlord' was given the designation Ninth Air Force, which had previously been used for the USAAF command in the Middle East. Physically this was a re-designation of the Eighth Air Force's VIII Air Support Command, taking all its combat units. Over the next eight months the Ninth Air Force grew to be the largest USAAF command of all, if only briefly. Its fighter arm eventually comprised three groups of P-38Js, two groups of P-51Bs and the similar C model, 13 groups of P-47Ds and two night fighter squadrons with P-61 Black Widows, these last not becoming fully operational until after the invasion of Normandy. The mighty Thunderbolt had been given improved low-altitude performance by a wide-blade propeller and water-injection equipment, the latter allowing short bursts of power that raising speed by some 10–20mph. If still no match for the Fw 190A or Me 109G in low-altitude performance, it had a firepower and load-carrying capability which made it the best fighter in the American arsenal for ground attack. Furthermore, its rugged construction and air-cooled radial made it far better suited to weathering small-arms fire than either the Mustang or Lightning with their vulnerable liquid-cooled engines; a single bullet in a coolant line could lead to engine seizure. Until D-Day Ninth Air Force fighters supported both Eighth and Ninth Air Force bomber missions and practised ground attack, often against specific targets in occupied countries.

Following the launch of 'Overlord' the Eighth and Ninth Air Force's seven P-38 groups carried out standing patrols over Allied shipping in the Channel, the aircraft's distinctive twin-

**Right:** Reducing the span of the Spitfire gave improved handling at low altitude, but by the spring of 1944 the ageing LF Mk VB model was confined to localities where enemy interceptors were unlikely to be encountered. Like many squadrons sent to northern airfields, when No 118 Squadron went to Orkney in March 1944 its Spitfire IXs were left in the south and LF VBs were used to guard the approaches to naval bases in the area. Exposing a plan view as it banks away, NK:H also presents the 170 Imp gallon 'slipper tank' used to increase patrol endurance. (USAAF)

**Right:** The first Spitfire with the new Rolls-Royce Griffon engine to enter operational service was the Mk XII, of which only 100 were built. The early-model Griffon was low-altitude rated and the first Spitfire XIIs had only a marginally better performance than the clipped-wing Spitfire V. The Mk XII also suffered from directional instability. Only two squadrons used the model operationally, Nos 41 and 92, being equipped in the spring of 1943. No 91 converted to the Spitfire XIV in March 1944 but No 41 soldiered on with Mk XIIs until September that year. Mk XII MB882/EB:B of No 41 Squadron is seen near Shoreham in April 1944 when the unit was based at Friston. The Griffon was a larger, heavier engine than the Merlin, requiring a redesigned cowling on the Spitfire. Operations by the two Spitfire XII squadrons were chiefly concerned with coastal shipping or interceptions of low-level, hit-and-run raiders. (IWM C20648)

**Above:** The first Tempest wing was formed at Castle Camps in April 1944 when No 486 Squadron converted from Typhoons. The Wing Commander Flying was the redoubtable Roland Beamont, who had returned to operations following a period as a Hawker test pilot. His personal aircraft, JN751 (marked R:B), is in the foreground as a No 486 Squadron Tempest V passes overhead on 8 April. 'Bea' Beamont used JN751 to shoot down an Me 109G near Rouen on 8 June 1944, the first Tempest air victory. Wing Commanders and ranks above were permitted to use their initials or a selected combination of identification letters on their personal aircraft. At the time this photograph was taken the Tempest still retained the special black and white type identity markings underwing that were inherited from the Typhoon. These were removed in April as it was planned to use similar markings for all tactical aircraft involved in 'Overlord'. (IWM CH13964)

**Right:** Convinced of the rocket projectile's destructive power, the RAF selected the Typhoon as the launch vehicle for these missiles in 'Overlord' ground support operations. No 609 Squadron, the only ex-Auxiliary Air Force unit to be equipped with Typhoons, was one of the first trained to use the weapon. Re-arming No 609's aircraft is taking place at Thorney Island in this photograph. JR379/PR:L, in the background, survived operational service with four squadrons to be sold for scrap late in 1945. (IWM CH13345)

boom configuration giving trigger-happy anti-aircraft gunners no excuse for opening fire. RAF Spitfires covered the bridgehead, while the long-ranged P-51s patrolled allotted areas further into France to intercept if the *Luftwaffe* put in an appearance.

P-47s carried out fighter-bomber missions, bomber support and sweeps. But on the morning of 6 June 1944 the *Luftwaffe* was conspicuous by its absence over the Normandy invasion beaches. Only two Fw 190s put in an early appearance, and it was not until later in the day that the *Luftwaffe* was encountered in any strength. Some 5,000 Allied fighter types were available, outnumbering their enemy six to one, but during the next few days transfers from the *Reich* raised the total in *Luftflotte 3*, the *Luftwaffe* command in France and the Low Countries, by another 600, although most of these were *Jabos*. While light flak—37mm and 20mm—and small-arms fire remained the principle nemesis of the ground attack fighter, the sheer nature of their work made the Spitfires, Typhoons, Lightnings and Thunderbolts particularly vulnerable to interception. Orbiting while waiting to be called in by an army unit, flying at reduced speeds and heavily laden with bombs or rockets, they had little time to evade if 'bounced' by Me 109s or Fw 190s. Cloud pervaded most days in June and early July, providing good cover for stalking the low-flying Allied aircraft. Losses were high. During the month following the D-Day landings in Normandy the Ninth Air Force tactical fighters suffered a total 248 missing in action, of which 44 were P-38s, 176 P-47s and 28 P-51s. One P-47 group alone lost 30 aircraft and pilots out of its complement of 70 during this period. On the other hand, *Jagdgruppen* sustained even higher losses, for any German aircraft that ventured over or near the bridgehead had only a 50/50 chance of surviving, such was the Allied air superiority.

Eight days after the invasion got under way the Germans began launching their V-1s, the Fieseler Fi 103 flying bombs, from the Pas de Calais area against London. Powered by a simple ram-jet, these small, winged missiles, with a 6m span, attained a speed of 400mph, making them difficult to overhaul and shoot down. Interception was best achieved with the latest Griffon-engined Spitfire, the Mk XIV, then equipping two squadrons, and the Hawker Tempest, both capable of speeds in excess of 440mph. The Tempest, which also equipped two squadrons at this time, was really what the Typhoon should have been three years earlier. A development of that aircraft, it incorporated a completely new wing with a laminar flow aerofoil, affording higher speed and better manoeuvrability. It was

**Left, upper:** Adjusting the rocket launch rails on Typhoon JP407. Each rail was marked with its position so as to ensure trouble-free re-fitting if removed. Each rocket weighed 90lb, of which 18lb was high explosive. Its propellant lasted 1.37 seconds and its velocity on impact was 800ft/sec.

This No 609 Squadron aircraft was shot down by ground fire near Laigle on 29 July 1944, the pilot, Flight Sergeant R. Ashworth, being killed. (IWM CH20558)
**Left, lower:** Adorned with special D-Day markings of black and white stripes, 4th Fighter Group Mustangs

prepare to take off from Debden at 1820 hours on 6 June 1944. In this view from the control tower 334th Fighter Squadron aircraft are on the runway, while those of the 335th Fighter Squadron wait to follow. (USAAF)
**Above:** The residue of war replaced

bathers on the beach at St Aubin-sur-Mer in June 1944. Included was P-47D 42-76297/D5:H of the 365th Fighter Group, here being examined by a GI. The Thunderbolt's engine was starved of fuel and the pilot had to make a hasty crash-landing. (USAAF)

powered by the same Sabre engine as the Typhoon, and high-altitude performance was poor.

A problem soon evident in shooting down V-1s was the danger to the assailant from flying debris and splinters if the 1,750lb warhead was detonated. The prudent pilot did not open fire from close range. An alternative method of dealing with a flying bomb entailed flight alongside, gently tipping it over with a wingtip under one of its wings. This action caused the directional gyros to unbalance and the missile to dive into the ground or sea. A total of 1,771 V-1s were brought down by fighters between 13 June and 9 September 1944, when the launching sites were overrun. Several men developed great skill in shooting down V-1s, the supreme champion being Squadron Leader Joe Berry, a Tempest pilot, who was credited with 60. Late in the campaign the RAF's first jet fighter squadron was brought into action, its Gloster Meteor Is accounting for several V-1s.

When in late July the US forces broke out of the bridgehead at St Lô and the *Wehrmacht* began to retreat, the Typhoon redeemed itself in the counter-attack at Mortain and the subsequent battle in the Falaise area. Using air-to-ground rockets, the Typhoon squadrons were primarily responsible for the mass destruction of armour and transport that occurred. Once the skill of aim had been mastered, the rocket became a far more accurate and effective means of destruction than fighter-bombing. This success was not achieved without substantial losses, almost all to ground fire, the Ninth Air Force's fighters keeping the *Luftwaffe* at bay. As the German 7th Army retreated towards the Rhine it was continually harassed by British and American ground attack aircraft—aircraft originally designed to meet a different requirement, i.e. aerial combat. The *Luftwaffe* also used an aircraft designed as an interceptor fighter as its main ground attack type—the Fw 190. These *Jabos* made valiant efforts to stem the Allied advance but were usually pounced on by British and American fighters. On two occasions Ninth Air Force P-38 units had considerable success against *Jabos* in low-level fights, where the Lightning proved able to out-turn the heavy Fw 190s.

**Above:** US Army engineers laying Square Mesh Track (SMT) on A-6 Beuzeville, the first American landing ground in Normandy to be completed and used by P-47s to re-arm and refuel. A Thunderbolt of the 406th Fighter Group can be seen on the left; at the time its home base was Ashford. (USAAF)

**Below:** Sherman tanks moving up to Tilly-sur-Seulles on 17 June pass a Spitfire of No 412 Squadron 'bellied in' by the road. Pilot Officer D. R. Jamieson's MJ136/VZ:S suffered a glycol leak and engine overheating on 10 June and he put the aircraft down in Allied-held territory. Many losses had nothing to do with enemy action. (IWM B5660)

**Above:** The flying strip at Beuzeville was 5,000ft long and 120ft wide with SMT surface support. It had 75 aircraft standings, two-thirds being SMT-covered. The fuel storage held 31,000 US gallons. The base was built by the 819th Engineer Aviation Battalion in ten days, being completed on 18 June. The Thunderbolt taking off to the south-west is an aircraft of the 405th Fighter Squadron, part of the 371st Fighter Group, which began moving into this site from Bisterne, England, as soon as A-6 was completed. (USAAF)

**Below:** Typhoon pilots at interrogation on the Normandy landing ground at B-2 Bazenville, which was used as a forward base from 13 June. (IWM CL164)

**Left:** Canadian Mustang pilots of No 414 Squadron enjoy a game of cards during a brief rest in a Normandy orchard at B-2 Bazenville ten days after the landings. Left to right are Flight Lieutenant J. T. Seaman and Flying Officers J. L. Rousell, L. F. May and J. G. Yougne. Later that day Lewis May's Mustang I was hit by flak, but he baled out successfully. (IWM CL166)

**Below:** A relaxed ACM Sir Trafford Leigh-Mallory, the Air Commander-in-Chief of the AEAF, talking with pilots of Colonel Gil Meyer's 368th Fighter Group at Cordonville airstrip. From being AOC Nos 12 and 11 Groups and Fighter Command, Leigh-Mallory's new command proved rather superfluous. When he was given a new post in the Far East the transport Liberator in which he was flying got no further than a French mountainside. There were no survivors. (IWM CH393)

**Right:** Among the many Polish airmen who gave such valued service to the RAF, Eugeniusz Horbaczewski was one of the most distinguished. As commander of No 315 Squadron, equipped with Mustang IIIs, he was leading a formation strafing enemy ground positions in Normandy on 22 June 1944 when another Mustang of his section, PK:J, flown by Warrant Officer R. Tamowicz, was hit by ground fire. Tamowicz was slightly wounded but managed to get his aircraft back into the beach-head area and crash-landed in a marsh. Seeing that Tamowicz had not left the cockpit, Horbaczewski landed on a nearby strip still under construction by US engineers. Going into the marsh, which entailed wading waist deep through water in some places, Horbaczewski released the dazed pilot from his safety straps and with the aid of the US engineers tended his wounds and got him to the landing strip. Having enlisted the Americans to help in getting Tamowicz into the cockpit of the Mustang, Horbaczewski climbed in and sat on his lap, started up and took off. The Mustang, FB166/PK:G, landed safely at Coolham, where ground crew were understandably surprised to see two men emerge from the cockpit. In this photograph, taken on 25 June, Horbacewski, with the aid of another member of the squadron, demonstrates how the rescue was

achieved. Horbaczewski was a member of the special Polish flight that operated in North Africa with Spitfire IXs in the spring of 1943, where he destroyed eight enemy aircraft in combat. He lost his life in a mass fight over Beauvais airfield on 18 August 1944 after shooting

down three Fw 190s. His total victory credits were 16, one shared aircraft and four V-1 flying bombs. (IWM CH13566)

**Below:** Typhoons of No 175 Squadron armed with rockets taxi out, cab rank, for another tactical operation from advanced landing

ground B-5 at Le Fresne. RAF Regiment gunners man the defences. Many of these sorties involved no more than five or six minutes' flying, the target often being so close to the front line that ground crews could see the Typhoons diving down to release their rockets. (IWM CL403)

**Above left:** Cricket in Normandy. Ground crews relax during an off-duty period at B-5 Le Fresne during the first week of July 1944 while others work on JR252 XP:M, a No 174 Squadron Typhoon that survived hostilities. This landing ground was shelled on occasions. IWM CL407.

**Left:** An RAF Repair and Salvage Unit work on a Mustang III, FZ190 of No 19 Squadron, at B-12 Ellon, Normandy. On the night of 15/16 July 1944 the airstrip came under very accurate fire from German artillery. Three ground crewmen were killed and all but four of the squadron's Mustangs damaged. For a while thereafter serviceable aircraft removed to B-9 at night. The service team are, left to right, Flying Officer F. H. Price, LAC L. Polley, Corporals J. Hughes and N. Lee, and

Sergeant. W. G. Ward. Note the generator lead plugged into the electric power pack. (IWM CL571)

**Above:** Armed Typhoons of No 245 Squadron take off from B-5 Le Fresne on 12 July 1944. The wet weather of June 1944 gave way to a period of very dry conditions the following month, with large amounts of fine soil particles turned to dust by 2,000hp engines. Special air filters had to be hurriedly obtained and fitted to prevent the damaging effects of this abrasive material on cylinders and pistons. (IWM CL449)

**Below:** Group Captain W. R. MacBrien RCAF, commanding No 127 Wing (Spitfires), watches as his Wing Commander Flying, Wing Commander James E. Johnson, greets Winston Churchill during the Prime Minister's visit to the

Normandy bridgehead. In the line with 'Johnnie' Johnson at B-2 Brazenville on 23 July 1944 are, left to right, Group Captain Paul Davoud, CO of No 143 Wing (Typhoons); the Wing Commander pilot of Churchill's VIP Dakota (name not recorded); and Squadron Leader E. P. Woods, CO of No 403 Squadron. (IWM CL512)

**Overleaf:** While French farmers start their harvest, a Spitfire of No 443 Squadron trundles past on a taxiway bulldozed through the wheat at B-3 St Croix-sur-Mer. This Canadian squadron was specially formed in February 1944 for 'Overlord' and the support of Canadian ground forces. (IWM CL614)

**Left:** Pierre Clostermann, the most successful French pilot flying with RAF fighter squadrons, was credited with 19 victories while flying Spitfires and Tempests in over 400 sorties. He returned to French soil in June 1944 with No 602 Squadron, based at B-11 Longues, near where this photograph was taken. One suspects that he had designs on some pâté de foie gras. (IWM CL553)
**Below:** The first purpose-built night fighter to enter service with the USAAF was the Northrop P-61 Black Widow. A somewhat ugly aircraft, it was a highly effective night-fighter once the usual crop of technical troubles that plagued most new designs had been overcome. Two independent squadrons, the 422nd and the 425th NFS, operated Black Widows with the Ninth Air Force in France. The aircraft was powered by two R-2800 radial engines and had a maximum speed of 360mph. The armament comprised four 20mm cannon housed in the underside of the fuselage behind the nose radar. This P-61B was visiting an Eighth Air Force bomber base in England, where it obviously caused great interest. (USAAF)

**Right:** Long-range fighter support in darkness for RAF Bomber Command was fraught with difficulties. Mosquitos were sent out on many occasions to try and intercept *Luftwaffe* night fighters leaving or returning to their bases. Wing Commander Norman Starr, with Pilot Officer J. Irvine, caught an unidentified enemy aircraft over Schwabish Hall, deep in Germany, on the night of 17/18 July 1944. Closing to 50yds' range, Starr fired and his target exploded, debris showering over the Mosquito and damaging its tail. The No 605 Squadron CO managed to nurse his aircraft back some 400 miles to Manston. Here the crew examine the tail damage to Mosquito VI NS690—in which part of the enemy aircraft was lodged—the following

day. Wing Commander Starr was yet another fine airman who lost his life in an aircraft accident, in his case as a passenger in a communications Anson when returning to Britain to get married. (IWM CE155)

**Below:** In the early summer of 1944 an improved model of the P-47D was reaching the squadrons. The internal fuel capacity had been increased by 65 US gallons, extending the radius of action, and a reduction in rear fuselage height with a 180-degree vision cockpit canopy improved the pilot's outlook. One of the first examples, resplendent in personal decor, was assigned to 56th Fighter Group ace Lieutenant Fred Christensen. There are 22 victory symbols on 42-26628/LM:C, *Rozzi Geth II*. (USAAF)

**Above:** The flying strip at A-29 St James was wide enough for two P-47s to take off together in echelon position. As the large nose of the Thunderbolt obscured the pilot's view ahead, an officer who was not flying waved off each pair as soon as the preceding element had left the ground. It was essential to get a squadron into the air and in formation as quickly as possible in order to respond to army requests for support. These 373rd Fighter Group P-47Ds have 150 US gallon drop tanks under the fuselage and a 500lb HE bomb on each wing rack. (S. Clay Collection)

**Below:** The losses of Ninth Air Force fighter-bombers attacking German ground forces were particularly high during the two months following D-Day. A number of unit commanding officers were among those killed or taken prisoner. Lieutenant-Colonel Robert Coffey, Executive Officer of the 365th Fighter Group, was one casualty: hit by ground fire on 11 July, he was forced to belly-land his P-47D, 42-26407/C4:Y *Coffey's Pot*, managing to get clear as it erupted in flames. Here he taxies out at Beaulieu a few days earlier. (USAAF)

**Above:** Raising dust despite a spraying with waste oil, a Lockheed Lightning of the 485th Fighter Squadron takes off from the landing strip at A-3 Cardonville, August 1944. The aircraft is a P-38J-20-LO model, 44-23520/7F:O. (USAAF)

**Below:** Two red-nosed Thunderbolts of the 63rd Fighter Squadron, 56th Fighter Group, head back to England over the Channel from a fighter-bomber raid in support of ground forces. The nearest aircraft still retains a 150 US gallon fuel tank under the belly. The Eighth Air Force had only four P-47 groups from June 1944, and these were increasingly used for ground attack missions as the bomber escort was taken over by the longer-ranged P-51s. (S. Clay Collection)

**Above:** Back home: a section of Thunderbolts arrives back at Boxted following a mission on 17 July 1944. The usual procedure was to swoop down towards the head of the runway in use and then make a banking climb to separate, curving round to lower gear and make a landing approach. The mechanics in the foreground are working on 42-26044/HV:<u>Z</u>, *Silver Lady,* the first bare metal-finish P-47 received by the 61st Fighter Squadron. (USAAF)

**Left:** The rocket-firing Typhoon proved to be a highly effective weapon and was largely responsible for the vast destruction of *Wehrmacht* armour and transportation that took place in the so-called Falaise Gap during August 1944. This gun camera frame shows rockets aimed at tank targets on a road at Livarot, 18 August. (IWM C4571)

**Above:** These beaming pilots of the 405th Fighter Group at Picaville took the surrender of over 300 German troops on 14 August. They had been strafing road transport north-east of Le Mans when they noticed a large body of enemy troops waving white flags. Circling, the Thunderbolt pilots saw that the Germans had formed a column. Radio contact was made with the US 7th Armored Division and the surrendering column was directed towards the American lines to be made prisoner. Responsible for this unusual feat were (left to right, front row) 2/Lt H. J. Morel, 1/Lt Joe R.Young and 2/Lt John Canfield, and (back row) Captain J. R. Willingham, the Flight Leader, and 2/Lts H. J. Presada and James P. Thomas. (USAAF)

**Above:** With generally little *Luftwaffe* daylight activity in the vicinity of the battle front, Allied interceptor units engaged in ground attack. The Spitfire, with its narrow undercarriage track, was not an ideal vehicle for hauling heavy loads from makeshift airfields, but even so the type was used quite extensively for fighter-bombing, usually with a 250lb or 500lb missile on the underfuselage rack. No 125 Wing squadrons flying the clipped-wing Spitfire IXE mounted both fuselage and wing racks, enabling each aircraft to carry one 500lb and two 250lb bombs on armed reconnaissance sorties. The wing was led by Wing Commander A. G. Page, seen here taxiing out at Longues on 20 July 1944 in his personal Spitfire marked with his initials 'AGP'. Geoffrey Page baled out of a flaming Hurricane during the Battle of Britain and was badly burned. He later commanded No 132 Squadron, which was part of No 125 Wing, and was credited with 11° aerial victories. (IWM CL726)

**Left:** The Lightning was frequently assigned to defensive patrols over Allied shipping off the coast of Normandy following the D-Day, the reason being its distinctive twin-boom configuration, which gave even the most trigger-happy naval gunner no excuse for a mistake in aircraft identification. This photograph was taken in August and shows a 367th Fighter Group P-38J high over shipping gathered near the mouth of the Seine. (USAAF)

**Above:** The dispersal area of the 492nd Fighter Squadron, 48th Fighter Group, at Deux Jaumeaux, early August 1944. The only weather protection for ground crews in what were once farm meadows was the small canvas 'igloo'. The jerrycans served to top up the P-47s' fuel tanks. (USAAF)

**Right:** In summer 1944 the Berger G-suit became available to USAAF fighter pilots. Its purpose was to limit blackouts in fast, tight manoeuvres, allowing pilots to make tighter turns in combat. Operated through the vacuum system, the suit inflated automatically under G-stress, placing pressure on the lower body and preventing excessive blood drain from the head. The pilot wearing the G-suit is Major Joseph Thury, CO of the 505th Fighter Squadron, 339th Fighter Group, based at Fowlmere. Joe Thury excelled at ground strafing and by the end of hostilities had destroyed 25 enemy aircraft on their airfields. (USAF)

**Left, upper:** No 122 Wing's Mustang IIIs were used for fighter-bombing and armed reconnaissance in support of the invasion forces until September 1944, when their true potential was realised by returning them to England to fly long-range escort for RAF Bomber Command. A load of two 1,000lb HE bombs was used on occasions, in this case to attack supply barges on the Seine, 6 August. Hoisting a bomb into position at B-12 Ellon with the aid of hand-operated winches are, left to right, Corporal W. H. Glover, LACs G. G.Hammon, C. B. Barrell, J. Taylor and A. Blundell, and Corporal S. R. Powell, all of No 122 Squadron. (IWM CL732)

**Left, lower:** During the four months of intensive activity following the Normandy invasion, some 200 RAF Typhoons were lost to enemy action, of which only 25 are known to have been shot down by enemy fighters; the principal cause was light flak and machine-gun fire from enemy ground troops. Canadian Pilot Officer C. E. Benn of No 182 Squadron was looking for enemy armour east of Vire on 7 August when his aircraft, JR427/XM:S, was hit by 20mm fire. The pitot head was shot away so that his speed instruments did not function, the oil tanks suffered shrapnel perforations and a 3ft hole was torn through the port wing. Undeterred, Benn pressed his attacks, claiming hits on a tank. His flight commander, Flight Lieutenant P. H. Strong, formated with the damaged aircraft and through radio contact arranged to fly alongside on the landing approach to their base at B-30 so that Benn could maintain the correct speed. After a successful landing it was discovered from two holes in the perspex hood that a flak splinter had passed between Benn's head and the armour plate, a separation of two inches! No 182 Squadron's CO, Squadron Leader G. J. Gray (right) congratulates Pilot Officer Benn for saving the aircraft. After repair JR427 was pensioned off to fly with No 56 OTU at Milfield. (IWM CL851)

**Right, upper:** Squadron Leader Johannes Le Roux was claimed to be the pilot who wounded Field Marshal Erwin Rommel, commander of the *Wehrmacht* forces in France. Flying Spitfire IX MK775 in the evening of 15 July 1944, he strafed a German staff car observed on a road south of Caen. Later in the month it was announced that Rommel had been wounded in the head when attacked by a British aircraft in that area on 15 July and had been returned to Germany. From South Africa, a nation that produced several high-scoring fighter aces, 'Chris' Le Roux had joined the RAF in 1939 and was a survivor of the decimated Fairy Battle squadrons committed to battle during the *Blitzkreig* of May 1940. In 1941 he was posted to No 91 Squadron and claimed six enemy fighters in as many months. Early in 1943 he went to North Africa and had further claims flying with No 111 Squadron. A third tour was in command of No 602 Squadron, and his air victories were increased to 18 and two probables. On 29 August 1944 he set off on leave from his Normandy base to fly to England in PL155 . The weather was bad and he turned back. The weather seemed better in the evening and he set off once more, never to be seen again. His usual Spitfire, MK144/ LO:R, was named after his wife. (IWM CL784)

**Below:** An improved version of the Griffon engine provided the Spitfire XIV with an excellent performance at most combat altitudes. The first squadron to receive this model, which was capable of 448mph, was No 610 in January 1944. RB159/ DW:D was the CO's aircraft. Squadron Leader R. A. Newbury had four enemy aircraft and eight V-1 flying bombs to his credit, several of the latter while flying DW:D. (IWM CH13816)

**Left, upper:** A Spitfire XIV about to tip a V-1 with its wing-tip. Most V-1s were shot down—a dangerous task. The most successful V-1 slayer was Squadron Leader Joe Berry, who brought down 60, all while flying a Tempest. (IWM 16280)

**Left, lower:** Another example of damage from an exploding victim. Disintegrating aircraft often posed a threat to the safety of their destroyer, in a few cases fatal. The wooden Mosquito was particularly prone to fire damage in such instances, as happened during the night of 10/11 August 1944 to the aircraft flown by Flight Lieutenant G. R. I. Parker with Flight Sergeant D. L. Godfrey. In the Le Havre region the crew first successfully attacked a Ju 88, then were vectored to another bandit which was identified as an Fw 190. 'Sailor' Parker—the nickname derived from his award of a DSM for service as an air gunner in Fleet Air Arm Swordfish and Fulmars earlier in the war—gave the Focke-Wulf a long burst, causing it to explode. Flaming petrol enveloped the Mosquito's tail, burning away much of the rudder fabric. The No 219 Squadron aircraft was returned safely to base at Bradwell Bay. (IWM CH13670)

**Right:** The distinctive nose radome covering the scanner of the AI Mk VIII radar in the Mosquito NF XIII. This particular aircraft is HK382/RO:T of No 29 Squadron at Hunsdon in January 1945. It was passed to No 409 Squadron, and its pilot lost control in cloud, resulting in a fatal crash near Lille on 16 March 1945. (IWM CH14647)

**Above:** Spitfire IXE VZ:H of No 412 Squadron sets out on 24 October along the brick-surfaced taxiway at Volkel airfield in the Netherlands. The aircraft is weighed down with a lethal cargo of two 250lb and one 500lb HE bomb, and the ground crewman seated on the wing acts as a guide in keeping the pilot 'on the hard'. The long nose of the Spitfire, as with all fighters of similar configuration, prevented the pilot seeing straight ahead—not a problem when the aircraft could be 'weaved' from side to side in forward motion, but this was not possible on narrow tracks. To wander off the hard into soft ground would almost certainly result in a nose-down. (IWM CL1451)

**Left:** While attacking three minesweepers off the Dutch coast on 2 November 1944 Flying Officer D. J. Butcher of No 3 Squadron sustained three cannon shell hits on his Tempest V EJ766/JF:V. One holed the rudder and jammed it, another hit the port wing leading edge and damaged the aileron so that the aircraft could only be turned in one direction, and the third entered the underside of the fuselage just behind the cockpit. Flying the damaged Tempest back to Volkel (B-80) and making a safe landing was no mean feat. (IWM CE163)

# 13
# ITALY AND THE BALKANS

Most of the army cooperation techniques employed by 2nd TAF and Ninth Air Force fighters in the summer of 1944 had been evolved in the Mediterranean campaigns the previous year. In Italy the winter stalemate in the hills south of Rome had resulted in increased tactical fighter activity and the re-equipment of many units. In the US Twelfth Air Force the P-40 Warhawks were replaced by hardy P-47D Thunderbolts for fighter-bomber work and the RAF's commands received Spitfire VIIIs and IXs in place of the remaining Mk Vs. The American Spitfire squadrons also received these more powerful models, but in the spring of 1944 they were transferred to the Fifteenth Air Force and re-equipped with P-51B Mustangs for use in escorting the Fifteenth's heavy bombers. Two other groups also received P-

51s, one of these the only negro-manned combat air unit in the USAAF. The three MTO P-38 Lightning groups were also transferred to the Fifteenth Air Force for escort and bomber support.

The P-38 was less troubled by extreme cold and humidity in the MTO. Technical improvements made for improved performance in high-altitude flight, if the limitations on diving remained. However, it was the P-51s that saw most of the air combat during support of B-17s and B-24s. The Lightnings

**Below:** Easter Service 1944 at Cuttela, conducted by Squadron Leader R. Davies of No 3 Squadron RAAF. Musical accompaniment is provided by a piano accordion while upturned tree stumps serve as an altar. The Kittyhawk II is FS449, which was later passed to the French. (IWM CNA1708)

were often diverted to fighter-bombing and ground attack, the most auspicious occasion being on 10 June 1944 when 46 set off from Italy to fly 550 miles to Ploesti, their mission to dive-bomb an oil refinery that had so far survived high-level bombing. Each P-38 carried one 1,000lb bomb and a 150 US gallon drop tank. They were accompanied by another group of 48 Lightnings which was to act as top cover while the attack was in progress. In the target area the force was intercepted by Fw 190s and, although claims of 23 shot down were made, 22 of the P-38s failed to return. The Ploesti oilfields provided about a third of Germany's oil requirements and the destruction of these installations became a major objective for the Fifteenth Air Force bombers, which eventually caused such devastation that production had all but ceased when the Russians captured the area in September 1944. The *Luftwaffe* concentrated its meagre fighter force in the defence of Ploesti and where possible avoided the P-38s and P-51s to concentrate attention on the heavy bombers.

The comparative dearth of *Luftwaffe* opposition to air activities over Italy meant that flak was the chief hazard for Allied aircraft. At low altitudes, when in known areas of flak concentration, the prudent pilot made a rollercoaster passage, continually changing height and direction. Cover of darkness

**Left:** Flying Officer Maurice Hayes rests in the shade of his No 3 Squadron RAAF Kittyhawk while waiting for another sortie to be called, October 1943. To increase the load on the Kittyhawk's single bomb rack two 500lb bombs were coupled together. (IWM CNA 1955)

**Below:** A four-cannon Spitfire VC of No 2 Squadron SAAF with a 500lb bomb, heading for the Sanrgo river battle front, spring 1944. A squadron emblem is painted on the rudder. (IWM CNA2109)

was used by the *Luftwaffe* for its offensive operations, particularly those ranging far beyond the front. The RAF had three night fighter squadrons in the area to challenge this activity, those equipped with Beaufighters having been withdrawn or converted to Mosquitos. The Twelfth Air Force also had four night fighter squadrons equipped with Beaufighter VIFs. The US crews had trained in Britain and had expected to use the type only until the dedicated American night fighter, Northrop's P-61 Black Widow, arrived. Production and development problems delayed the appearance of the P-61, so that late in 1944 one squadron converted to Mosquitos, another retained the Beaufighter to the end of hostilities and the other two squadrons finally received Black Widows during the final months of the war after moving to France. The only other notable equipment change was in RAF fighter squadrons where Mustang IIIs replaced Kittyhawks from the second half of 1944. The Mustangs were employed for both ground attack and long-range offensive sweeps or bomber support over the Balkans. Most of the Mustang units eventually specialised in the use of air-to-ground rockets, weapons which had proved their worth with the Typhoon squadrons in western Europe.

As the ground front moved up the Italian peninsula, part of the Twelfth Air Force was detached to operate from southern France following the Allies' almost unopposed invasion in August 1944. The fighter element, chiefly P-47 groups, became part of the provisional 1st Tactical Air Force, which also embraced a number of French Spitfire IX- and Thunderbolt-equipped units, the Spitfires meeting the air defence requirements. The 1st Tactical Air Force also received two P-47 groups from the Ninth Air Force in order to fulfil its duties with ground forces advancing up the Rhône valley.

**Above left:** Mechanics changing a tailwheel on 315th Fighter Squadron P-40F 41-13903/48 of the 315th Fighter Squadron discuss a problem with others. Some of the men have taken advantage of the tailplane to obtain some shade from the summer sun. The rough landing grounds from which fighter-bombers usually operated were not kind to tyres. (S. Clay Collection)

**Below:** No 32 Squadron dispersal area at Foggia Main in March 1944. The squadron had a mixture of Spitfire HF.VIII and F.IX models, the former used for high-altitude interceptions, albeit that these were few. JF404/GZ:M is a Mk VIII in an azure blue finish, as is GZ:B; GZ:D/MA802 is a Mk IX in normal day camouflage. A Battle of Britain squadron, No 32 was sent to Greece later in 1944 and in November was stood down, there being more fighter squadrons in the MTO than was deemed necessary with so little aerial opposition. (IWM CNA2663)

Major Eric M. Baker, the 25-year-old CO of No 5 Squadron SAAF with his personal Kittyhawk FR781/GL:H (named *Raynor* after his wife), which he used for nearly all the sorties of his second tour, amounting to some 200 hours in five months. Although most of Baker's sorties were ground attack he also made claims of three enemy aircraft shot down. The other officer is Lieutenant W. A. Gillham, Squadron Engineering Officer. The bomb in the foreground is a 1,000lb HE. (IWM CNA2491)

The scoreboard reads:

213 Sqd.
SCORE CARD

| | FINITO | PROBABLE | DAMAGED |
|---|---|---|---|
| | 6 | 2 | 5 |
| | 4 | | 11 |
| | 136 | DAMAGED | |
| | 28 | | |
| | 60 | | |
| | 7 | | |
| | 5 | | |

PREVI. SCORE 203

**Left:** The scoreboard of No 213 Squadron gives a good indication of the dearth of enemy aircraft in the MTO during the final year of the war. Service in the Battle of Britain and the Middle East brought 203 air claims, but only four were shot down over the Balkans. The 136 locomotives give the squadron's Spitfires' and Mustangs' main line of employment in that area. (IWM CNA4314)

**Right:** Fighter units of the Fifteenth Air Force were detached from strategic operations to support the invasion forces in southern France using Corsica as a forward base. Here P-38 pilots of the 94th Fighter Squadron relax in a building commandeered for a barracks at Poretta. Drop tank packing cases have been used to fashion a table; candles provide the night-time illumination. (USAF)

**Left:** In August 1944 the Allies' invasion of southern France met little resistance. *Luftwaffe* air opposition was also limited, and the wing of RAF Spitfires moved to Ramatuelle to provide daylight air cover was soon able to return to Italy. One of the squadrons was the famous No 43, which had served with Fighter Command during the Battle of Britain, at this time equipped with Spitfire IXs and some of the high-altitude-rated Mk VIIIs. In this photograph, taken on 22 August, one of the latter is being serviced soon after arrival at this French airstrip. (IWM CL998)

**Below:** The USAAF had no night fighter units on entry into the Second World War. Experience was had from the RAF, who trained four American squadrons in England and equipped them with Beaufighters. All four entered combat in the MTO and by the end of hostilities had a combined total of 71 enemy aircraft credited as destroyed. The 415th Night Fighter Squadron flew the Beaufighter VIF from June 1943 to the end of the war in Europe, having 21 victories; contacts were far from plentiful. V8899, used by this squadron, is seen here at Dijon Longvic in September 1944. This Beaufighter was also used by an RAF night fighter squadron in Italy for a time. (S. Clay Collection)

**Above far left:** A Lightning that certainly paid its way for Uncle Sam. P-38F-15-LO 43-2136 started out in North Africa and flew 143 operational sorties, 45 of which were fighter-bombing. Three enemy aircraft were claimed by its pilots. The veteran was photographed at the 1st Fighter Group's base at Vincenzo, Italy, shortly before its retirement. (USAF)

**Left:** Kittyhawk squadrons were being re-equipped with Mustangs as these became more plentiful during the final months of hostilities. No 3 Squadron RAAF was one of these, its Mustangs seen here at Fano amongst the detritus of war on a rainy day. (IWM CNA4901)

**Above:** No 6 Squadron was one of the last operational units in the Mediterranean theatre to fly Hurricanes, first having received the type early in 1941. By the end of hostilities it was flying Mk IVs from Prkos, Yugoslavia, with four rocket rails under one wing and a 44 Imp gallon auxiliary fuel tank under the other. The additional fuel was required for ranging patrols looking for enemy transport and shipping. (IWM CL3480)

# 14
# STRATEGIC FIGHTER DOMINANCE

By midsummer 1944 the Eighth Air Force had ten of its fifteen fighter groups equipped with Mustangs. In late May the first examples of a new model, the P-51D, had reached the squadrons. The main visual difference was the so-called 'bubble' cockpit, giving the pilot an excellent all-round view. This was achieved by reducing the rear fuselage spine; this adversely affected directional control until a small forward expansion of the fin at its base was added to mitigate this tendency. The P-51D also featured a welcome increase in firepower with an armament of six .50-calibre weapons, whereas the P-51B and C models had but four. The plan was to convert the remaining fighter groups to Mustangs eventually, but at this time, owing to losses, wastage and the demands of other forces, this excellent aircraft was in short supply, so much so that later in the year the complement of squadrons had to be reduced from 25 to 20 machines. Nevertheless, up to 500 P-51s were regularly despatched on long-range missions during the summer of 1944, often of four or five hours' endurance and sometimes of as much as six or more, made possible by carrying two 108 US gallon capacity drop tanks. These latter were increasingly the paper/plastic type made in Britain.

The major strength of the *Jagdflieger* was forced to concentrate within the borders of the *Reich*, and, with a belated if significant increase in fighter production, depleted units were being replenished and new units formed. For, in spite of all the destruction wrought by Allied bombing, German aircraft production concentrating on fighters had reached an all-time high, even if the majority were upgraded versions of the trusty Fw 190A and Me 109G. The *Luftwaffe* may not have been lacking fighters but it was most certainly short of competent fighter pilots. Many of the *Experten* had fallen during the great air battles of the spring and replacements lacked training and often good leadership. The most critical shortage was fuel, since with the loss of the Ploesti oilfields and the concerted Allied bombing campaign against the synthetic oil plants in the *Reich*, supplies dwindled at an alarming rate. Oil industry

installation attacks nearly always brought a spirited defence and both Eighth and Fifteenth Air Force fighters could expect to meet the *Jagdflieger,* although the former saw most of the action.

The *Jagdflieger* tended to conserve forces and only on chosen occasions rise in strength to contest the American daylight raids during the latter half of 1944. The intention was to inflict such heavy losses during a single day's operations by the Eighth Air Force that the Americans would be forced on to the defensive. The first of these major efforts was against just over a thousand B-17s and B-24s sent to attack synthetic oil plants on 11 September. An estimated 500 German fighters rose to challenge the Americans and had to contend with an almost equal number of P-51s in the course of destroying 39 of the bombers. The Mustang pilots were credited with 115 enemy fighters shot down, the highest total claims for a day's operations so far—this against seventeen of their own, plus eight crash-landings due to damage in friendly territory. One of the P-51s was lost in a collision and three as a result of ground strafing activity, for which claims of another 42 enemy aircraft were made. Several of the Americans made multiple credits, three pilots with four each and seven with three—an indication of the lack of training and poor quality of many of the *Luftwaffe* pilots encountered. From the summer months and through to the end of hostilities this was a not infrequent occurrence, and a number of Mustang pilots were credited with five in a day and one 'ace' six. In all cases the P-51s had intercepted large formations of enemy fighters where their victims often made only feeble attempts at evasive action.

The following day, when the Eighth Air Force again visited the oil industries, the *Luftwaffe* also rose in some strength, but was obviously weakened by recent losses. The Eighth Air Force fighters claimed 54 air victories and 26 by strafing airfields at a cost of twelve Mustangs. Losses of 35 bombers were, as on the previous day, concentrated in individual group formations, the result of the most successful of all forms of attack devised by the *Jagdflieger*. Heavily armed and armoured Fw 190As

**Above:** A Type 16 high-definition radar station used to direct fighter aircraft to enemy formations within a range of 120 miles from its coastal site. A more advanced control system, Microwave Early Warning (MEW), which had a range of 200 miles, was used on the Continent from the autumn of 1944. (IWM CH15204)

**Right:** P-38Js of the 364th Fighter Group in battle formation over East Anglia. The J model had intercooler radiators removed to beneath the Allison engines and 55 US gallon fuel tanks placed in their former position in each wing. This gave the Lightning a much better radius of action, allowing flights as far as Berlin. Unfortunately, the new model did not overcome the low temperature problems which caused so much trouble for the Eighth Air Force groups. (USAAF)

flying at *Staffel* or *Gruppe* strength carried out a mass pass while shielded above by substantial numbers of Me 109Gs. These attacks were usually mounted on formations where the German raid monitoring organisation had detected a lack of escort. The Fw 190s of the so-called *Sturmgruppe*, weighed down with armour plate and heavy 30mm cannon, were handicapped in escape or in defending themselves if intercepted by P-51s, incurring severe losses on such occasions.

By November *Luftwaffe* single-engine fighter numbers were in excess of 3,000 and on the 2nd another deep penetration of enemy airspace by American bombers to strike at the Merseburg/Leuna synthetic oil plants saw a further display of strength by the *Luftwaffe*. Once again the P-51s made this a costly business, and although the *Jagdflieger* and vicious flak claimed 40 bombers the American fighters believed that 102 German aircraft had fallen; the true figure, about 60, was still a substantial loss. Thereafter another lull indicated that the *Luftwaffe* was again conserving its forces and fuel for massive trials of strength. They came on 21, 26 and 27 November, again in the defence of oil. The Eighth Air Force fighters claimed 68, 114 and 98 air victories against 15, 9 and 15 losses. On 5 December the *Luftwaffe* did its best to protect Berlin and suffered claims of 91 for 17. In all cases the true losses were somewhat lower, despite much more careful pilot interrogation and study of gun camera film. What the numbers did reveal was the scale of fighting and a five- or six-to-one advantage for the Eighth Air Force: the air supremacy achieved in the spring was not only being maintained but gathering advantage.

Some of this advantage could be ascribed to technical improvements introduced during the late summer. The first was the 'Gee suit', pilot torso air bands that inflated automatically when high gravitational loads were induced, preventing loss of blood from the brain and 'blackout'. Gee suits allowed tighter turns or pull-outs in air fighting. The other technical advance was the K-14 gun sight. Based on a British design, this gyroscopic device enabled very accurate deflection shooting, hitherto a matter of personal skill. The British lead in radar development extended to improved ground control for di-

**Left, upper:** Captain Robert S. Johnson climbing into his P-47D, 42-76234/HV:P, at Boxted, 25 April 1944. At the time he was the leading air ace in the ETO with 25 victories, which he increased to 27 the following month. A later reassessment put his total at 28 destroyed. He was an excellent marksman, and all but two of his victories were obtained with the 61st Fighter Squadron, which also produced the other top-ranking ace of the ETO, Francis Gabreski. (USAAF)

**Left, lower:** Charles Leonard, assistant crew chief (left), and Sergeant Harvy Weber, crew chief (on far wing), assist Lieutenant Charles Yeager settle in the cockpit of his P-51D named after his wife. Yeager was shot down in February 1944, evaded capture and returned to the 357th Fighter Group at Leiston later in the summer. On 27 November 1944 he claimed four enemy fighters, bringing his total claims to 11½. This pilot was to make his mark in history post-war as Chuck Yeager, the first man to exceed the speed of sound. (M. Olmsted Collection)

**Left:** Captain Jack Ilfrey, about to set off on another mission from Kingscliffe, poses beside his personal P-38J, 43-28341/MC:O. 'Happy Jack' came to Britain with the 1st Fighter Group in 1942, and, notwithstanding his landing in and escaping from neutral Portugal, became one of the first P-38 'aces' when the group moved to North Africa. He returned to the United Kingdom with a number of other P-38 pilots to build experience in the 20th and 55th Fighter Groups when they arrived with Lightnings in the later half of 1943. (S. Clay Collection)

recting offensive fighter operations. The MEW and Type 7 systems were taken to the Continent and frequently used to vector Allied fighters towards enemy formations in hostile airspace at ranges of up to 150 miles.

However, in the light of the aviation advances being introduced by the Germans at this time, British and American progress in this field appears extremely limited. Allied intelligence had been aware of the development of jet-propelled aircraft for some time, if not the pace of progress. In July 1944 USAAF pilots encountered the Me 163 rocket-propelled fighter, which impressed with its acceleration and speed (well in excess of 550mph). It was soon realised that this little swept-wing aircraft had a very limited endurance and once its fuel was spent had to glide down to earth. Because of their speed Me 163s were able to strike at Allied aircraft with some immunity from interception. A few were themselves shot down by Mustangs, but the threat of large-scale employment never materialised as the unstable nature of the rocket fuel made their operation exceedingly hazardous: pilots were more at risk from an explosion than from Allied fighters.

A more menacing appearance, the following month, was that made by the Me 262, powered with two turbojets. With a top speed of 540mph and armed with a nose battery of four 30mm cannon, this was a formidable opponent. To work out the best tactics in combating the *Luftwaffe* jets, the USAAF used P-51s in trials with RAF Meteors. It was clear that the only way the Mustang could come near to overhauling an Me 262 was in a dive, and then only if the jet was flown in a curving course. Appreciating that the jet would have a limited endurance and that because of the specialised fuel it would normally use a limited number of airfields, the plan was to identify these bases and by patrols attempt to catch the Me 262s on take-off or landing when they were at their most vulnerable. When practised this proved reasonably fruitful, with Mustangs destroying several of the aircraft in these circumstances. However, failure of the Jumo 004 engines was not uncommon, and a number of Me 262s were shot down when lacking power.

In the autumn of 1944 the Me 109K and Fw 190D were coming into service in small numbers. The former was a higher-powered and more heavily armed version of the G model. The Fw 190D had a Junkers Jumo 213 liquid-cooled engine in place of the air-cooled BMW radial, giving higher speed, particularly at altitude. There were some performance advantages over the Mustang, but these were insufficient to make an impact in countering the loss of air superiority.

While the RAF had earlier had no call for a long-range fighter, by the summer of 1944 there had been a change in policy. The six squadrons that the RAF had been able to equip with Mustang IIIs were assigned to the 2nd Tactical Air Force and operated in a fighter-bomber role for several weeks. With the liberation of most of France and the withdrawal of the *Jagdflieger* into the *Reich*, RAF Bomber Command decided to turn part of its force to daylight operations in precision attacks on targets in the Ruhr. Escort was required, and the Mustangs were withdrawn from the 2nd Tactical Air Force to provide this. More Mustangs being made available, two wings of eventually ten squadrons were formed for this purpose and based in East Anglia. Unlike the Eighth Air Force fighters, their sorties did not take them far enough into Germany to encounter the huge formations the *Luftwaffe* occasionally launched against raiders. Mustangs were also used to provide escort and local support for Coastal Command Beaufighters and Mosquitos striking enemy shipping off Norway. RAF Fighter Command, a title restored in October 1944, eventually had twelve squadrons of Mustang IIIs and IVs, the latter being the British designation for the P-51D.

**Left:** The much improved P-51D model Mustangs began to reach the ETO in late May 1944. These featured an increase in armament from four to six wing-mounted .50-calibre machine guns and a 'full view' cockpit canopy made possible by a reduction in rear fuselage height. The P-51D in the photograph, 44-13857 of the 374th Fighter Squadron, 361st Fighter Group, was shot down by flak while fighter-bombing near Orléans on 13 August 1944. The pilot, 2/Lt Loren Montgomery, survived. (USAAF)

**Right:** The celebrated Colonel Donald Blakeslee, ex-RAF Eagle Squadron ace and commander of the 4th Fighter Group during its most successful period with the Mustang. An excellent pilot and air leader, and noted for exceptional navigation skills, Don Blakeslee led the first fighter 'shuttle' mission from England to the USSR. (USAAF)

**Left:** Blue-nosed Mustangs of the 486th Fighter Squadron, 352nd Fighter Group, stand ready nursing 108 US gallon drop tanks at Debden, June 1944. On the 21st they joined the 4th Fighter Group in providing escort for B-17 Fortresses undertaking the first 'shuttle' mission to the USSR. From Russia they escorted the bombers to Italy and then back to Britain—a round trip of some 3,000 miles (I. Swerdel)

**Left:** Sergeant Thurman Winfield replenishes the ammunition bay of a 78th Fighter Group P-47D at Duxford. The trace was made up alternately with two armour-piercing incendiary and three incendiary rounds at this time, June 1944. The quantity of ammunition per gun varied depending on range requirements, but 425 rounds was the maximum. (USAAF)

**Right:** On 18 August 1944 the 479th Fighter Group, the last Eighth Air Force unit with P-38 fighters, carried out a strafing raid on Nancy/Essay airfield, where a great many *Luftwaffe* aircraft, mostly bombers, were found. The 50 Lightnings proceeded to make several passes over this lightly defended base, claiming 43 aircraft destroyed and 28 damaged. This is a gun camera frame from Lieutenant Harold Greening's P-38 showing his fire being steered towards an He 111. (USAAF)

**Below:** A red-nosed 334th Fighter Squadron Mustang reposes in a German farmer's field, 12 September 1944. Captain Tom Joyce found his engine overheating and had to belly-in near Darmstadt, He became a POW. (S. Clay Collection)

**Above:** Perhaps the most eye-catching of all fighter group markings employed by USAAF units flying in Europe were those of the Fifteenth Air Force's 325th Fighter Group, self-dubbed the 'Checkertail Gang'. The group's Mustangs featured bright yellow and black empennages. This 318th Fighter Squadron P-51D, with the strange nickname *Stout Burr-Bon,* nurses two 75 US gallon drop tanks as it flies over the eastern Alps. The Alps were beautiful to see but no place to be in an ailing aircraft. (S. Clay Collection)

**Below:** Scarlet tails identified the Mustangs of the only USAAF combat air unit with negro personnel. The 332nd Fighter Group, serving the Fifteenth Air Force for fighter escort duties and based at Ramitelli, Italy, was also unusual in having four instead of three assigned squadrons. (S. Clay Collection)

**Above:** S/Sgt Alfred Morris prepares to close the canopy of Captain William Mattison's P-51C at Ramitelli, Italy. The squadrons of the 332nd Fighter Group were credited with a combined total of 108 aerial victories by the end of hostilities. (USAAF)

**Right:** Major Herschel Green (left) was one of the top fighter pilots in the MTO. He had 18 air victories with the 317th Fighter Squadron, three while flying P-40s, ten with P-47s and five flying P-51s. (S. Clay Collection)

**Above:** By the autumn of 1944 the USAAF had dispensed with its operational training establishments in England and Northern Ireland. Thereafter each Eighth Air Force fighter group carried out its own theatre indoctrination for pilots with a number of aircraft retired from combat use for instruction in combat flying techniques. Permission was given for the conversion of two war weary P-47s or P-51s to carry a passenger, achieved by moving radio equipment further aft. This P-47C 41-6258/A:J is an example of a two-seat conversion and was used by 65th Fighter Wing headquarters as a fast communications aircraft. (USAAF)

**Below:** The K-14 computing gun sight was introduced progressively in operational P-47s and P-51s from August 1944 and fitted to production models from early 1945. Based on the British gyroscopic Mk 11C model, it allowed very accurate deflection shooting and was praised by American pilots as a significant aid to their trade. (M. Olmsted Collection)

**Right:** The legendary 'Hub'. Colonel Hubert Zemke was considered the best leader in VIII Fighter Command by its commander, Major-General William Kepner. He led the famous 56th Fighter Group, dubbed 'Zemke's Wolfpack', which 'showed the way' in taking on the *Jagdflieger*. An amateur boxer, the aggressive Zemke encouraged a competitive spirit among his own pilots which spread to the other fighter groups of the command. In August 1944 'Hub' moved to take command of the youngest group in the Eighth Air Force, the 479th. On what was literally his last mission before leaving for a staff appointment, his P-51D—that seen in the photograph—broke up in a storm over Germany. Zemke finished the war as the senior Allied officer in charge of Stalag Luft I. (USAAF)

**Above:** Captain Glenn Eagleston, an original pilot of the first P-51B-equipped group, the 354th, in the cockpit of his Mustang at Orconte, France, November 1944. By the end of his second tour Eagleston had 18½ air victories to his credit, a total higher than that of any other Ninth Air Force pilot. He was a member of the 353rd Fighter Squadron, the highest-scoring fighter squadron in the USAAF. (S. Clay Collection)

**Below:** Strafing was a dangerous business but this rarely dissuaded Eighth Air Force fighter pilots from seeking targets of opportunity after finishing their escort duties. Lieutenant-Colonel Bert Marshall was shooting up a troop train when his Mustang was hit by 37mm fire from a mobile flak battery. Marshall brought the fighter back over Steeple Morden only to discover that loss of hydraulic power prevented the main landing gear from lowering and he was forced to make the third belly landing of his operational career. The photographer caught the Mustang moments before it impacted the runway. P-51D 44-14798/WR:B, *Jane IV*, had some 200 perforations. (S. Clay Collection)

**Right:** Handsome Major George Preddy relaxes at a press conference at the Pentagon during home leave. 'Ratsy' Preddy was, in terms of enemy aircraft shot down, the most successful Mustang pilot, with 25 and four shared victories. His record included the unsurpassed six Me 109s on one mission when his group, the 352nd, came upon a huge enemy formation assembling for an attack on heavy bombers on 6 August 1944. Tragically, Preddy was killed by fire from a US Army anti-aircraft battery while in a low-level pursuit of an enemy fighter on Christmas Day 1944. (USAAF)

**Above:** Most drop tanks used by the Eighth Air Force during the final months of the war were made in Britain. The compressed paper/plastic 108 US gallon model was the most common type used on Mustangs, being extremely light to handle. Wright Field tested them and advised the Eighth Air Force that they were unsuitable for operational use—this when the number already employed on long-range missions was in five figures! The tanks were apt to develop leaks if not handled carefully. (USAAF)

**Below:** The Mustang's long legs: the stockpile of 108 US gallon drop tanks at the 55th Fighter Group base at Wormingford. Those with silver finish are the Bowater paper/plastic composition type. The dull grey-painted tanks are steel and were prefabricated in Britain. (R. Sand)

# 15
# THE LUFTWAFFE'S LAST THROES

On 16 December 1944 the *Wehrmacht* launched a major counter-offensive in the west, with armoured columns striking through the Ardennes forests just as had been done so successfully in 1940. A period of extremely poor weather had been chosen, to minimise the Allied response in the air, and indeed heavy cloud, mist and rain persisted for a week then turned to frost and snow. When the weather did clear sufficiently for the Allies to bring the full weight of their bombers to bear they were met with strong opposition from the *Jagdflieger*. High totals of Allied claims of over 400 enemy aircraft destroyed between 22 and 31 December, even if exaggerated, apparently did not dissuade the *Luftwaffe* from its New Year's Day enterprise. Catching the Allies completely off guard, some 800 German fighters took part in a large-scale, low-altitude sweep to strafe and bomb RAF- and USAAF-held airfields. Maintaining complete radio silence, the *Jagdgruppen* attacked sixteen airfields in the Low Countries and

one in France, destroying 127 aircraft (six in the air) and damaging 111. This would have been a significant achievement had it not been for the losses incurred, which amounted to 270 Me 109s and Fw 190s, including several of the new 109K and 190D models. Additionally, 40 of the fighters that did regain German-held territory had damage. Most of the *Luftwaffe* losses were to ground fire; some were due to the Germans' own anti-aircraft defences.

The *Wehrmacht*'s ground offensive was soon halted, not least by fuel shortages, and the territory lost regained. Fuel supplies had been a growing problem for the *Luftwaffe* during the second half of 1944, and it was now necessary to restrict operations in order to conserve supplies. Following the 1 January débâcle little was seen of the *Jagdflieger* for a fortnight. Then, when on 14 January the Eighth Air Force struck again at oil, large numbers of enemy fighters were put into the air. The day's fighting produced the largest air claims ever for the

**Right:** The only US Ninth Air Force airfield that suffered severely from the *Luftwaffe* strike on New Year's Day was Metz, where the 365th Fighter Group had a score of its Thunderbolts destroyed or damaged. The smoke from three burning P-47s is visible in this wintry scene. (USAAF)

**Left:** During the large-scale *Luftwaffe* attack on Allied airfields on New Year's Day 1945, 364 aircraft were originally claimed as destroyed and 81 as probably destroyed; of this number 155 were shot down. As always, the number proved to be an overestimate, but the *Luftwaffe's* losses were still substantial. Four No 403 Squadron Spitfire XVIs setting out on patrol encountered a large number of Me 109s and Fw 190s attacking their airfield, B-56 Brussels/Evère. The Candians shot down six, three falling to the guns of Pilot Officer Steven Butts' RR526. One of Butts' victims crashed into a house in Brussels and disintegrated. (IWM CL1761)

**Right:** More destruction on New Year's Day 1945—but this occurred in England. A B-17 Fortress that had taken off from Bassingbourn suffered mechanical failure and attempted a crash-landing at nearby Steeple Morden, home of the 355th Fighter Group. The Fortress crashed on an aircraft dispersal area and exploded, wrecking P-51D 44-14374/WR:A and seriously injuring a crew chief. The B-17 crew were all killed. (S. Clay Collection)

American fighters, 155 against nine P-51s and two P-47s. One 48-strong group of Mustangs was alone credited with 55, having come upon formations of Me 109s whose pilots appeared to have little experience in handling their aircraft, let alone in air combat. Indeed, such was the critical shortage of fighter pilots that new recruits were being assigned to active units with a minimum of training. Many of the new pilots now came from bomber, reconnaissance and other units.

Not until 2 March, when another effort was made to protect the battered oil industry from the US bombers, was there much opposition to the Eighth Air Force from the *Jagdflieger*. Yet again the result was along familiar lines, with 66 German fighters shot down for the loss of thirteen Mustangs. At this time the Eighth Air Force had only one group retaining the Thunderbolt, and this had just re-equipped with the P-47M model, basically as the late P-47D apart from having a more powerful version of the R-2800 engine. In fact, at high altitude, the P-47M could attain 470mph and was thus faster than the Mustang. Unfortunately the new engine had not been properly protected for shipment overseas and a number of failures were traced to this neglect. Nearly every original engine had to be changed before the P-47M was cleared for full operational use.

The chief concern of the Allied air forces was the prospect of an increase in the number of German jets, particularly the Me 262 with its formidable armament of four 30mm cannon. The destructive nature of the 30mm rounds, particularly those used by the MK 103 weapon which were longer and had a larger explosive charge, was evident from the damage sustained by B-17s and B-24s fortunate enough to be able to return to base. The Me 262 also employed underwing batteries of 5.5cm rockets for assaults on the bomber formations. From observations by Allied pilots it was clear that the Me 262 was slow to accelerate and had a wide turning circle, weaknesses of which full advantage was taken whenever the opportunity allowed. By the end of hostilities some 100 Me 262s were claimed shot down, 60 of these by Eighth Air Force Mustangs. The Me 262 pilots had as their first priority the destruction of Allied bombers and were mostly vectored to the B-17 and B-24 formations. The usual form of attack was in three-plane flights, accelerating in a long dive to build up sufficient speed to outwit the escort and then opening fire from the rear with a level approach. The 300mph difference between attacker and target bomber and the high rate of closure did not bode well for accurate sighting, resulting in many near-misses. The number of Allied aircraft shot down by the German jets was not high—around 150—in spite of the latter's advantages and they had little effect on the conduct of the Allied air offensive.

As expected, the Allied crossing of the Rhine on 24 March 1945 generated increased *Luftwaffe* activity, with more examples of poorly trained pilots. As the ground forces pushed further into Germany a last effort in some numbers was made against the American bombers. On 7 April *Luftwaffe* fighters engaged in the only known case of organised ramming. Even that was not particularly fruitful, with only seventeen B-17s

and B-24s lost from all causes that day and American fighters claiming 64 of their opponents. Thereafter few *Luftwaffe* fighters sought combat and the Eighth Air Force P-47s and P-51s proceeded to seek out airfields on which to shoot up every cross-marked aircraft seen. Without fuel available these aircraft posed little risk, but no chances were to be taken. From 9 April to the 17th, when these attacks were halted, 1,697 *Luftwaffe* aircraft were considered destroyed and another 997 damaged; 724 were destroyed and 373 damaged on 16 April alone.

As usual, ground strafing took a steady toll, particularly when anti-aircraft defences were alerted. The previous year a defined method of strafing airfields had been established in order to keep exposure to the ground defences to a minimum. If aircraft were observed on an enemy base from high altitude, the American fighters were to continue on their way for not less than ten miles, observing prominent landmarks as they went. When sufficiently far away from the target to be out of view from that point, two or three flights would descend to low level, leaving one flight to act as top cover. The strafing contingent would then fly back towards the target, getting as low as safely possible and spreading out in line abreast. It was hoped that their approach would have the element of surprise, and after carrying out a strafing pass the attackers were to continue low until well away from the airfield. Unless the defences were found to be weak, a second pass was not advised. A later tactic, when aircraft were seen on an airfield, was for the squadron leader and his wingman to dive down to make a pass, drawing ground fire to determine whether the base were heavily defended. If not, then the rest of the unit would be called down; if the defences were heavy it was a case of leaving well alone. It has been estimated that for every fighter shot down in air combat, six were lost to ground fire.

In the final weeks of the war in Europe some *Jagdflieger* units still found the fuel and courage to fight on, despite the overwhelming odds against them. For the Allies the possibility of a last desperate massing of jet fighters was a concern, but this never materialised. The RAF moved Meteor Is to the Low Countries in April 1945 with the express purpose of intercepting *Luftwaffe* jets. Apart from a little ground strafing the Meteors saw no combat before the official end of hostilities on 8 May. The last air claim against the *Luftwaffe* was made that day when a US tactical reconnaissance Mustang had a combat with an Me 109.

**Right:** An officer of RCAF No 126 Wing looks across the airfield at Heesch (B-88) towards dispersed Spitfires of No 412 Squadron. Nos 411 and 442 Squadrons were also based on this Dutch airfield in January 1945. (IWM CL1889)

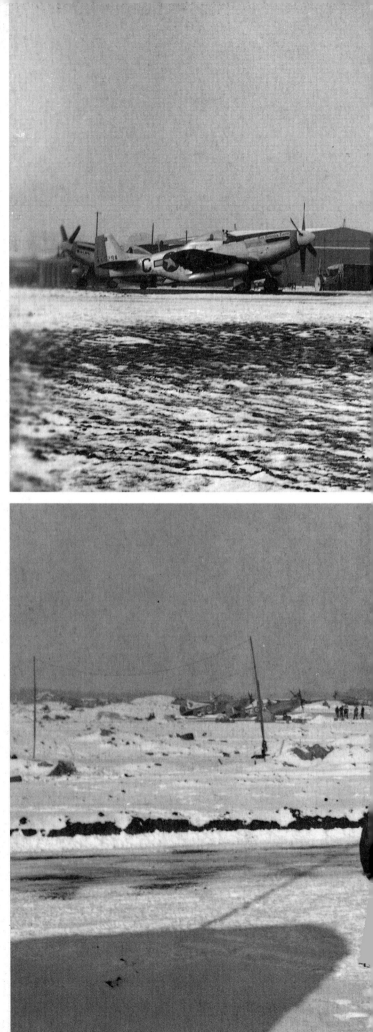

**Left:** *Worry Lamb, The Buckeye Flash* and 358th Fighter Squadron compatriots sit at snowbound Attlebridge waiting for the weather to clear at home base. January 1945 saw some of the coldest weather in England this century; flying conditions were often treacherous. (S. Clay Collection)

**Left:** Hard times for 'erks'. Snow and frost made maintenance and repair a miserable experience on exposed airfields. These men have removed the propeller from battered Typhoon QC:G of No 168 Squadron at B-78 Eindhoven, 10 January 1945. (IWM CL1799)

**Below:** The standard US Army high shoe did not provide much warmth in winter and a lined over-boot was a useful addition. Here 2/Lt Alfred Schroeder gets ready to enter the cockpit of 315th Fighter Squadron P-47D 42-28567/63 at Luneville for a strafing mission in February 1945. His crew chief holds the Form 1 maintenance record. The red diamond on the engine cowling identified the squadron within the 324th Fighter Group; the group's marking is the red lightning stripe. (USAAF)

**Above:** 314th Fighter Squadron P-47D 42-27113/36, armed with two 500lb HE bombs and six rockets, is directed out from its standing at the 324th Fighter Group base at Luneville, France, 2 March 1945. The fighter was despatched on a patrol in the US 7th Army sector in south-east Germany, with a mission to attack rail traffic. Held in three-tube clusters, the 4.5in rockets were an adaptation of an infantry weapon and proved rather erratic in flight. The weight of the explosive charge was 5.3lb, less than a third of that in the highly successful British air-to-ground rocket. (USAAF)

**Below:** Several French air units were activated in North Africa for service in the Allied cause. A *Groupe de Chasse* was the equivalent of an RAF squadron, and six were eventually equipped with P-47D Thunderbolts. As part of the 1st French Air Corps in the 1st Tactical Air Force, they supported the US and French ground forces in the drive through Alsace into Germany. This is a late production P-47D operated by *Groupe de Chasse I/5 Champagne.* It has a dorsal fillet added to the fin to give better directional control, which was adversely affected by the removal of the high fuselage spine when the P-47 was redesigned to have a 360-degree view cockpit canopy. (ECPA)

**Above:** *Tempus Fugit*, Colonel William Daniel's personal Mustang, put down on Torretto airfield in an emergency. The panel removed from the wing root suggests a coolant leak, a not infrequent problem with the lines that ran between radiator and engine. Daniel, a five-victory ace, was the last wartime commander of the 31st Fighter Group, the first USAAF fighter organisation to enter combat against the Axis in Europe. (S. Staples)

**Below:** Ready to go: pilots in the cockpits of 55th Fighter Squadron Mustangs at Kingscliffe await the scheduled time to start engines before a mission. Canopies were always kept open, to allow the pilot a quick exit in case of an engine fire on starting. (USAAF)

**Above:** Fully loaded and grossing nearly six tons, P-51D 44-63747/C5:C of the 364th Fighter Squadron pulls away from the Leiston runway at 95mph, February 1945. With the engine at 3,000rpm and pulling 61in of manifold pressure, this was a critical time for the pilot, who knew that any faltering in engine power could bring a fatal crash. The tailwheel is retracting, indicating that the gear-up lever has been actuated to reduce airflow drag as quickly as possible. With a load of 485 US gallons, 216 of which was in the two drop tanks, a radius of action of some 700 miles was possible. (USAAF)

**Below:** Mustangs maintained an indicated air speed of between 160 and 180mph on the flight out to rendezvous with the bombers they were assigned to escort, climbing steadily so that at least 25,000ft was reached by the time they were crossing into hostile airspace. The formation was closely spaced, about 25yds apart, during the flight out, as with these 20th Fighter Group P-51Ds high over the North Sea. (S. Clay Collection)

**Left:** On entering hostile airspace the squadron formation spread out over a two-mile front, line abreast, with each aircraft approximately 75–80yds from the next, as with this 356th Fighter Group P-51D, 44-15590/PI:M, at 30,000ft over Germany. (H. Rutland)

**Below:** A P-47M of the 62nd Fighter Squadron over a patchwork of fields in south-east Suffolk. All 108 production aircraft of this model Thunderbolt were assigned to the 56th Fighter Group at Boxted. Basically a P-47D airframe with a more powerful engine, the R-2800 C-type, it could top 470mph at 30,000ft, making it the fastest propeller-driven USAAF fighter in operational service. This particular aircraft, 44-21228/LM:K, is carrying smoke-dispensing tanks on underwing racks. The airfield in the top left of the picture is Raydon. (USAAF)

**Left:** 'Eager El'. Lieutenant-Colonel Elwyn Righetti, CO of the 55th Fighter Group, did not arrive in England until the autumn 1944 after commanding a US training establishment. He proved to be a brilliant and aggressive fighter leader, destroying 7½ enemy aircraft in the air and 27 on the ground at a time when the *Luftwaffe* was often conspicuous by its absence. Additionally his gun camera film recorded the blasting of some 50 locomotives and numerous other ground targets. Probably the most accomplished American strafer flying in the ETO, near the end of hostilities he was forced to crash-land his Mustang after it was hit by ground fire. Apparently escaping unharmed, he was never seen again, believed lynched by irate German civilians. (USAAF)

**Below:** A silver Mustang IV, the British designation for the P-51D and K, flying over Kent in February 1945. By 1945 RAF Fighter Command had followed the lead of the USAAF and dispensed with camouflage finishes on its American-built acquisitions. Mustang FH765/HG:R is a No 154 Squadron aircraft flown by Pilot Officer Palmer. (P. Knowles)

**Above:** Captain Ray Wetmore was credited with 21¼ air victories during 142 sorties with the 359th Fighter Group. Only one other pilot of the 400 who flew with this group at some time while it was combat-operational between December 1943 and May 1945 had claims in double figures. Wetmore's achievement was attributed to a combination of extraordinarily sharp eyesight and good marksmanship; it is said that he often reported enemy aircraft long before other members of his squadron saw them. Ray Wetmore was killed post-war in a jet crash. (USAAF)

**Above right:** The standard 150ft-wide runways on most British airfields allowed two single-engine fighters to take off together and, to hasten assembling a squadron formation, all aircraft were marshalled at the runway head. The form of marshalling varied from unit to unit. Mustangs of the 357th Fighter Group at Leiston were usually angled at 45 degrees so that pilots could see up the runway and quickly swing into a take-off position when their turn came. (M. Olmsted)

**Right:** RAF Mustangs of the Peterhead Wing, lined up each side of the runway, are signalled off by the controller. (S.Clay Collection)

**Right:** Several RAF fighter squadrons were re-equipped with Tempest Vs during the final months of hostilities, including No 33 Squadron, which had earned fame in the Middle East during 1940. With No 222 Squadron, it was sent to Gilze-Rijen (B-77) in February 1945. Led by No 33's CO, Squadron Leader I. S. G. Matthews, it flew its first sorties with Tempests on the 25th when a *Staffel* of Me 109s was seen in the vicinity of Rheine. Four of the enemy were confirmed as shot down, but in the fight one of the squadron's Tempests was lost (the pilot was taken prisoner) and Flight Lieutenant Leslie Luckhoff's aircraft, EJ880/5R:R, was hit in the fuselage, damaging the controls. 'Lucky' Luckhoff had been responsible for the demise of two of the Messerschmitts and while dealing with the second he had been attacked by another. After inspecting the damage the South African pilot was off to England to marry a WAAF. (IWM CL2318)

**Below:** Enemy anti-aircraft artillery and small-arms fire did not lessen in the last days of hostilities, as evidenced by Squadron Leader J. C. Doyle's damaged Kittyhawk FT928 at Cervia airfield, Italy. On 18 April 1945 Doyle, CO of No 450 Squadron, led a section flying a fighter-bomber patrol in attacking houses occupied by enemy infantry in the Bastia area. His Kittyhawk was hit in the fuel tanks, wing root and empennage, requiring great skill on his part to return safely to base. (IWM CNA3543)

**Above:** Meteor III EE234/YQ:O of No 616 Squadron, the only RAF jet fighter unit to see action during the war, takes off from Melsbroek, Belgium, in March 1945. The aircraft still retains the overall dull white finish applied when the first Meteors arrived on the Continent during snowy weather. The squadron had no contact with enemy fighters and only engaged in offensive sweeps and ground strafing. Fortresses and Mitchell bombers can be seen in the distance and a mobile Chance Light directional beacon stands in the foreground. (IWM C5658)

# 16
# THE RECKONING

During the Second World War the RAF lost approximately 10,000 fighter-type aircraft to all causes in action against Axis forces in Europe and the Mediterranean areas of operations. The USAAF lost some 12,528 to combat and accident, 5,107 of these in the MTO. British casualties amounted to 3,600 fighter pilots killed and the American loss of life was 3,950 in the ETO and 1,789 in the MTO. However, these figures are at the best arbitrary.

A large proportion of these losses were due to ground fire when fighter aircraft were employed in ground attack, for during the six years of hostilities aircraft designed for air combat replaced the dedicated ground attack designs. Indeed, towards the end of the conflict some were being utilised for operations that a few years earlier would have been undertaken by light bombers. This was the beginning of the trend which would eventually see the fighter assume an all-purpose combat role in the final years of the century.

Back in 1939 the fighter was viewed primarily as a bomber destroyer; combat with enemy fighters was at first a secondary consideration. As explained, the enterprising German aviation industry received considerable encouragement from the

**Below:** Several Ninth Air Force group commanders followed the custom of RAF wing and higher command officers in using their initials on personal aircraft. Colonel George Bickell, who commanded the pioneer USAAF P-51B group, the 354th, carried GR:B on Mustang 43-6877—although on the right side the 'GR' was carried forward of the national marking, in the fashion of standard squadron lettering. This P-51B was converted to take a passenger behind the pilot in the spring of 1944 and on 4 July was used by Major-General Elwood Quesada of IX Fighter Command to fly General Eisenhower over the Normandy battle lines. Thereafter the aircraft carried the name *The Stars Look Down*. (Cary Salter)

Nazis and in many areas had a three- to four-year lead on British and French designs and products at the outbreak of war. The British, in particular, had made some effort to meet the challenge, and it is evident that, generally, they did not appreciate the superiority of the only *Luftwaffe* first-line fighter, the Me 109E, until 1940. Not only was this cannon-armed aircraft as fast as, or faster than, the Spitfire I in level flight and superior in rate of climb, it normally had no difficulty in out-diving the best RAF fighter. This last factor was the most advantageous performance quality in fighter combat, and one that would hold true throughout the war. Even fighter types with mediocre level speed, climb and manoeuvrability could succeed if able to out-dive the opposition, for this gave the ability to overtake or outrun. Neither the Spitfire nor the Hurricane could out-dive the Me 109, and this was the *Luftwaffe* fighter's prime advantage over the British types. The platitudes of experienced Allied pilots later in the war held true throughout: 'Altitude is advantage'; and 'Nine out of ten fighter pilots never saw what hit them.' Striking from above with the element of surprise was the trademark of the *Jagdflieger* in the knowledge that their quarry was unlikely to dive away to safety.

Thus, better equipped, better armed and with better combat tactics, the *Jagdflieger* had little difficulty in cutting a swath through the brave opposition of Polish pilots in outclassed aircraft, or later the defensive efforts of the Dutch and Belgian Air Forces. The *Armée de l'Air* was a tougher opponent, even if many of its fighters were verging on obsolescence. RAF Hurricane pilots did their best, but the superiority of the *Jagdflieger* in equipment and overwhelming numbers could not be countered. Even so, a great many Me 109s were shot down in combat during the Battle of France, for, depending on circumstances, the inferior *can* score over the superior.

The propaganda of the day led the British nation to believe that Fighter Command had achieved a great victory during the Battle of Britain. A sober analysis would see the outcome as more a deliverance than a victory, with neither side defeated and the *Luftwaffe* failing to give Hitler the dominance of the sky desired before an invasion of England. Again, the Me 109 proved superior if its losses are the yardstick of assessment with those of the Spitfires and Hurricanes fought. 'The Few' are deserving of even more praise in view of the fact that they fought the *Luftwaffe* hordes with weapons inferior to those of the enemy.

The period following the Battle of Britain is the most sorry episode for Fighter Command. Because of the RAF's desire to take the offensive, fighter sweeps over the French coast became a frequent undertaking. Although these flights often incurred losses, Fighter Command believed that the claims of enemy fighters shot down more than matched the casualties.

The fact was that these claims were often twice to four times the actual losses of the *Jagdflieger*. Throughout the war all sides were faced with overstated claims: the sheer nature of air fighting—speed of combat, the pilot's restricted outlook, confused reactions, two or more pilots shooting at the same aircraft, misinterpretation of gun camera film—played a part in this, despite the best efforts of intelligence staff to establish a true picture. The cross-Channel forays gave the *Jagdflieger* the advantage: they chose the opportune time to attack from high altitude and refused to be drawn into turning combats. With the Spitfire V the RAF was confident that they had an aircraft that was a match for the Me 109F, introduced to operations around the same time, even though this new model had the same advantages over its adversary as the 'Emil'. Not until the Fw 190 appeared on the scene later that year was there recognition of the inferior performance of the Spitfire. A more powerful engine was hurriedly found for the Spitfire, but it was not until the following summer that the Spitfire IX became operational and then only in relatively small numbers. While the problems facing Britain from 1940 were many, air superiority being the key to all other offensive air operations, it is inexplicable that the upgrading of the Spitfire's performance was not pursued with the utmost urgency. As a result of this lethargy or indecision British fighter pilots were condemned to this unequal combat situation for the best part of two years—albeit that, as a result, for some time the *Luftwaffe* saw no urgency for replacements or upgraded versions of the Me 109 or Fw 190.

An even worse situation existed in the Western Desert, where Me 109s made easy pickings of Hurricanes, the best that Britain could offer until well into 1942. Here the RAF flew in support of the Army, and low-flying aircraft involved in tactical reconnaissance or fighter-bombing were particularly vulnerable to the more agile Messerschmitts. Not until the appearance of a goodly number of Spitfire IXs in 1943 was there an Allied superiority fighter in this area, although by this time the *Luftwaffe* had lost out to the RAF and USAAF through strength of numbers.

Both the *Luftwaffe* and the RAF held that a single-seat, short-range interceptor would always be superior to any long-range fighter development. Ironically, it was the British who had a fighter that would prove this false produced in the USA and then failed to recognise its potential. Nor initially did the USAAF, despite a growing requirement for long-range support of its day bombers, hopes being directed towards the P-38 Lightning which, in the event, proved disappointing in high-altitude operations over Europe. But it was the large P-47 Thunderbolt that first brought success in long-range escort, achieved with jettisonable fuel tanks. Having an inferior performance in many respects to the Me 109 and Fw 190, it did excel at high-altitude level speed and, more importantly, it could out-dive the enemy which, as the *Jagdflieger* had proved in the past, was a trump card in successful air combat. Somewhat to the surprise of both the RAF and the *Luftwaffe*, this giant among single-engine fighters suited its employment well. The Thunderbolt's thirsty appetite, limiting its radius of action, was the main reason it was superseded by the Merlin Mustang as an escort fighter. With jettisonable fuel tanks the Mustang could go anywhere the bombers went and take on the enemy at any altitude. From the spring of 1944 it was primarily the Mustang pilots who achieved what was unthinkable a year earlier—air superiority over the enemy's homeland. Nor had this been a strategic aim: it had come about primarily because of the necessity to protect the USAAF's heavy bombers, which had as a first objective the destruction of the enemy aviation-related industry by bombing. It soon became evident that neutralising enemy air power was fast being achieved in the air, so VIII Fighter Command was turned loose to hunt the *Luftwaffe* in the sky and on its airfields. The fighter was being used as an offensive weapon.

With no requirement for long range, RAF Fighter Command had to watch their American allies take the daylight offensive to the enemy. At night there could be no escort for RAF Bomber Command and only limited support by fighter intruder operations. In night defence the developments in AI radar had taken the interception of raiders from a near hopeless task to one where 9 per cent of *Luftwaffe* sorties over Britain were successfully intercepted. More than half RAF Fighter Command's first-line strength was taken into the 2nd Tactical Air Force for the cross-Channel invasion, where the American requirements were met by the Ninth Air Force. In these forces fighters combined air defence with ground attack, practising the art of army support which had been perfected in North Africa. The mighty Thunderbolt proved an excellent aircraft in this role and the once-disappointing Typhoon redeemed itself as the foremost slayer of enemy armour. The fighter had evolved into the most effective all-round ground support aircraft.

As for the fighter pilot, from experience in Spain the *Luftwaffe* pilot was trained in better tactics and was generally more proficient than his adversaries during the early years of the war. RAF training produced excellent fliers if initially pursuing obsolete tactics, and when success was achieved it was often due to personal prowess. That stated, in contrast to the *Luftwaffe*, which encouraged the creation of *Experten* and ex-

**Right:** RAF Fighter Command would soon be an all-jet force. Molesworth, a US Eighth Air Force bomber station for three years, was taken over by No 1335 Conversion Unit, the first for jet fighters, in the summer of 1945, with Meteors gliding along perimeter tracks that had said farewell to Fortresses only a few weeks earlier. (IWM 16363)

posed them to national acclaim, the RAF had no time for ace status and early in the conflict rarely allowed successful fighter pilots to be named, believing that this mitigated against team spirit. This attitude was to change, and only because of the Americans' lauding of individuals. The USAAF was quick to acknowledge personal achievement in shooting down enemy aircraft, seeing this as a morale builder both within the service and for the American public. Moreover, it was seen as combat encouragement and taken further in allowing individual units to be publicised, with the top score of enemy aircraft destroyed the target for other units to better. There is no doubt that this had a significant effect on building *esprit de corps*. Kudos was also given for the dangerous task of ground strafing enemy airfields, with aircraft destroyed thereon considered equal to air victories as far as Eighth Air Force public relations was concerned.

Generally, fighter pilots respected their opponents, even if in the national interest admiration for or sympathy towards the enemy should not be expressed. There were certainly those pilots who expressed hatred for the enemy, usually through some personal experience, but these individuals were a minority. Incidents of shooting at airmen descending by parachute have been levelled at fighter pilots of both sides. While there were a few individuals who did not want their adversaries to live and fly again, most of these incidents can be attributed to an aircraft firing at another the parachutist did not observe. There were also many reported cases of the deliberate strafing of civilians by *Luftwaffe* and Allied pilots. The fact is that the pilot of a fighter travelling at 200–300mph at tree-top height has little chance of distinguishing between military and civilian garb. If over enemy territory there was usually no hesitancy about shooting at a supposed legitimate target.

Both British Commonwealth and United States fighter pilots were well trained and committed to operations for specified periods. *Luftwaffe* pilot training fell away, so that with the attrition of the early months of 1944 the *Jagdflieger* units often consisted of a few *Experten* leading an inadequately trained majority. Bad-weather training was particularly poor and often kept *Jagdflieger* units on the ground. The result of this lack of training caused the decimation of many *Luftwaffe* formations encountered by Allied fighters. There was apparently an attempt to keep the neophyte fighter pilots well away from the battle fronts until some experience had been gained. Unfortunately for the *Luftwaffe*, no area of the *Reich* was immune from trespass by Eighth Air Force Mustangs.

A noticeable aspect of air fighting was the very high totals of aircraft shot down by *Luftwaffe Experten*. In the first instance this can be attributed to individual skills making use of the Me 109's advantages over its opponents, most noticeably the ability to out-dive: the hit-and-run tactic paid great divi-

dends. This was particularly so when the RAF took the offensive and the *Jagdflieger* did not have the handicap of escort or support for other task forces. Even so, the majority of these high totals were built on the Russian Front, where in the early days Soviet aircraft tended to become cannon-fodder through being of inferior performance and committed with little concern for survival tactics. As Allied air power burgeoned so the *Jagdflieger* was rarely short of quarries, whereas many British and American fighter pilots flew a combat tour and never saw an enemy aircraft they could engage. With no shortage of fighter pilots from 1942, it was Allied policy to give as many men as possible combat experience, frequently taking the most successful to pass their knowledge to others in operational training units. Few *Luftwaffe* pilots had such rest postings during the same period and eventually it was a case of flying until one became a casualty.

A proven tenet of warfare by 1945 was that air superiority was essential to the satisfactory pursuit of offensive action on land, sea or air. The Allied fighter pilots paid dearly for their respective governments' early neglect in providing the means to achieve this goal. That it was eventually reached and held was, in the final analysis, down to the man in the cockpit. He did not lose his status as the twentieth century knight.

**Below:** Douglas Bader was not long out of prison camp before he had acquired a Spitfire IX marked with his initials and was heaving his legs into the cockpit. This occasion is to lead the Battle of Britain celebratory fly-past over London in September 1945. (IWM CH16284)